Looking for Mies

Ricardo Daza

Looking for Mies

ACTAR Barcelona, New York

It is more than likely that this is not the first time we have seen this particular photograph or another one very like it.
Mies van der Rohe standing on the flagstones of one of his American buildings.
He puffs on a cigar, hand in pocket, eyes fixed on some distant point. Behind him, a glass wall; divided and subdivided by the metal frame bearing the frosted panes of glass and by the slats of the louvered blinds. Completing the composition, above, a strip of ceiling and, to the left, the blurred branches of a tree on the other side of the blinds. I found this photograph in number 8 (1956) of the magazine *Architectural Forum*. Without Mies' presence the scene would lack interest. Yet, on perceiving the disquieting figure of the maestro, one can't help asking oneself about the precise spot Mies chose that day to have his portrait taken in by Bill Engdahl, one of the photographers of the Hedrich-Blessing studio.[1]

Where is
Mies van der Rohe?

➡ He's doubtless in one of his own buildings.
His presence and the metal and translucent glass of the curtain wall bear witness to this.
Although the photograph only shows us the inside of the building, we may assume – thanks to the transparency of the curtain wall – that its appearance is practically the same on the outside.
A rapid glance at the buildings constructed by Mies with this kind of framework identifies the building.

No doubt about it, this is the Crown Hall building.

The building had been planned and constructed by Mies between 1950 and 1956 as the headquarters of the Chicago Architecture and Town Planning Department, part of the Illinois Institute of Technology.

In the Crown Hall building the entire outer skin (the front, rear and two side facades) consists of the repetition of a rigid 10-foot module between metal pillars.

What the photograph shows us, then, is the inner face of two of the modules which make up the facade.

But if the whole Crown Hall perimeter is formed by the repetition of that same module, Mies can be situated anywhere within the building.

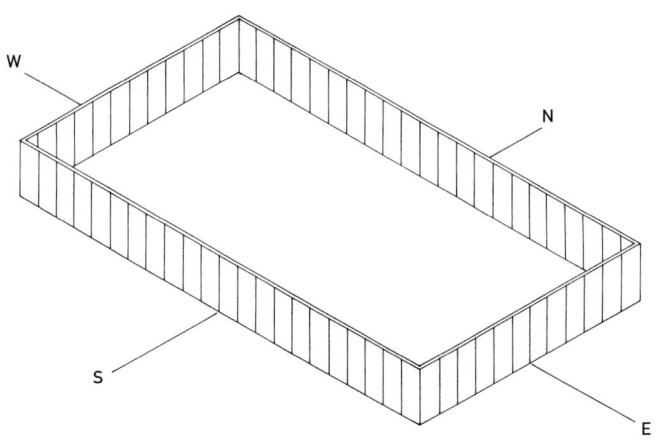

Where is Mies van der Rohe?

➔ Let's consider the strip of frosted glass.

It doesn't go all around the building. In order to hold up the roof of the building Mies used four extended metal colonnades, supported externally and 60 feet apart.

The entrances to the building, on both the south and north facades, are sited between two central colonnades.

There, in the six central modules of the south and north facades, the frosted glass panes were substituted by transparent glass and no blinds were positioned in the upper part.

The photograph shows us Mies in front of a wall consisting of frosted glass and blinds.

We can affirm, therefore, that Mies is in some part of the building apart from the six modules corresponding to the south entrance and the six modules corresponding to the north entrance.

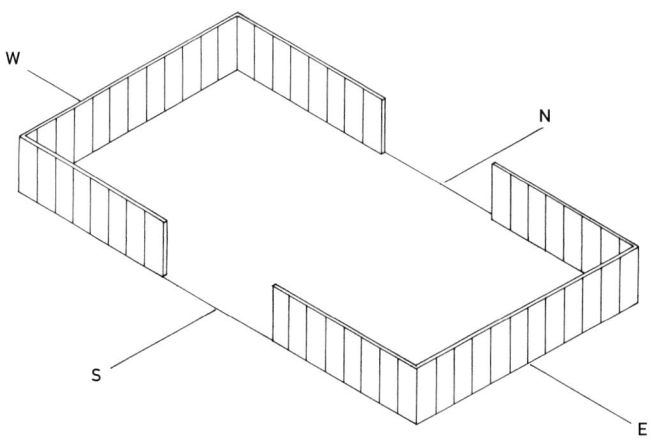

Where is Mies van der Rohe?

➜ Let's now focus on the metal upright dividing the photograph in two.

The metal structure of the Crown Hall building, designed by Mies and the engineer Frank J. Kornacker, consists of two kinds of pillars, each one placed towards the outside of the building.
The eight thicker ones support the four structural beams; the sixty-four thinner ones lend rigidity to the metal box.

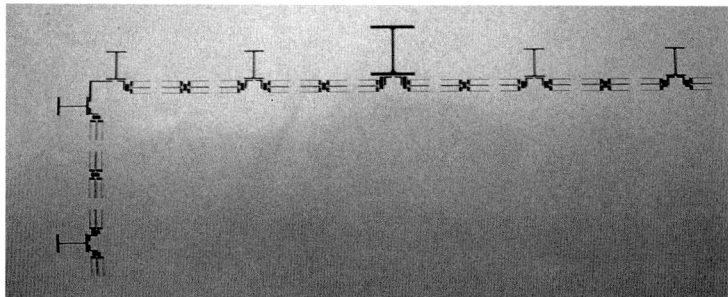

There can be no doubt about it, the metal support the photograph shows us is supported on the back of one of the thinner pillars. All one has to do is check the construction details.

If the upright in the photograph had been supported on one of the thicker pillars, we'd see, behind the open louvered blind, the left edge of the pillar, since its thickness is greater than the thickness of the uprights, while the thickness of the thinner pillars and the uprights of the window frame is practically the same.

We can check this feature thanks to the position in which Bill Engdahl placed his camera. Engdahl aligned the center of the lens with the axis of the metal upright. And so Mies can be in any part of the building except for in front of the south and north entrances or in front of the eight thicker pillars supporting the main joists.

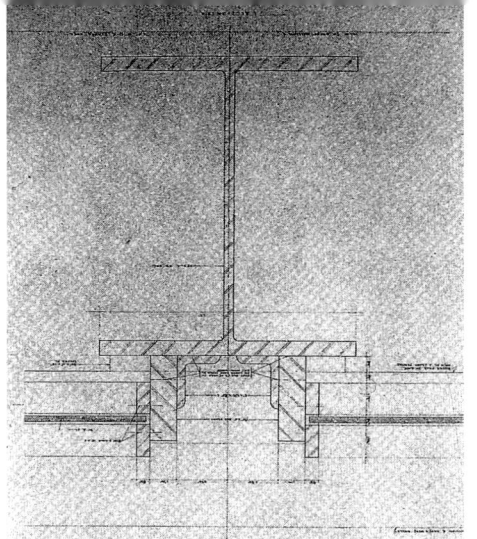
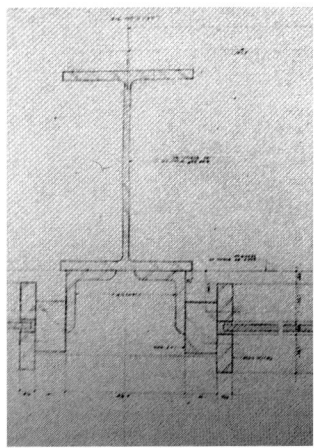

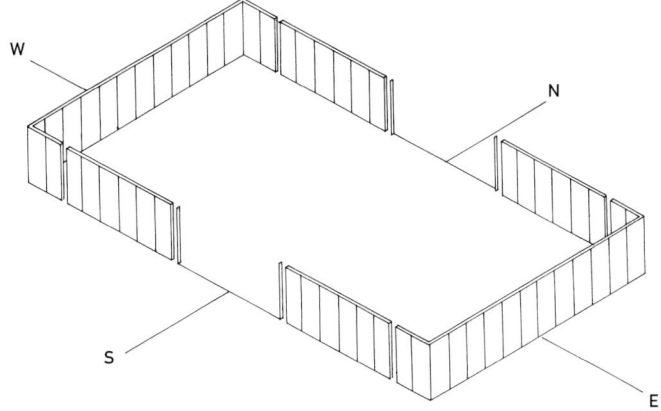

W

N

S

E

Where is Mies van der Rohe?

→ Let's go back to the photograph. To the left side of it.
Behind the open blinds the fuzzy branches of a tree, or their shadow, can
be made out very close to the facade.
Would Mies have thought about the siting of the trees?

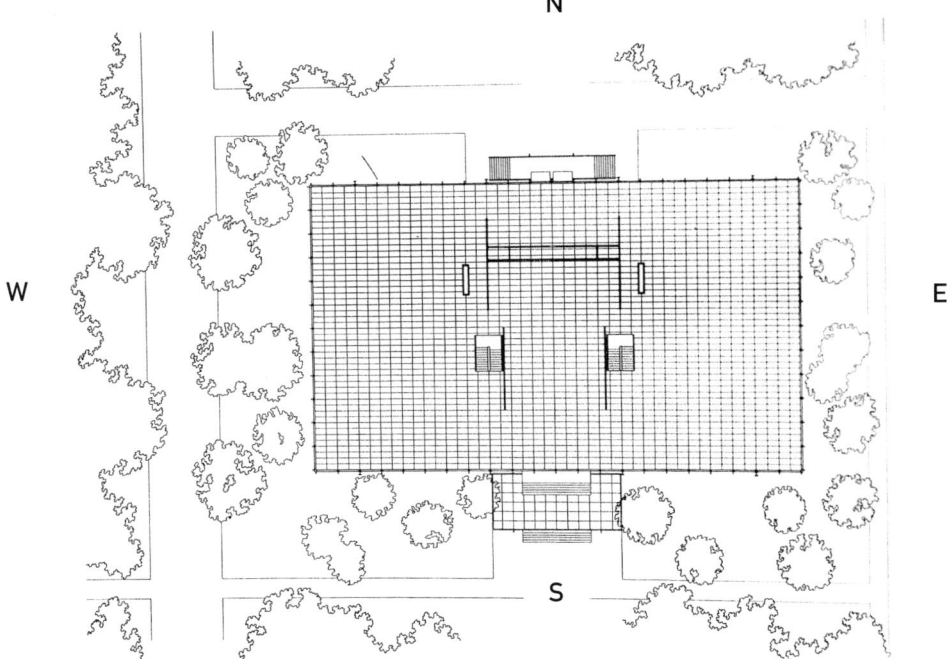

Let's look at a drawing of the Crown Hall floorplan.
On the west, east and south sides there are trees very close to the facade. On the other hand the trees on the north side are somewhat distant, and not very well defined.
We might venture, then, to reject the north facade as a background to our photograph. The tree or its shadow would not be seen so close to. Nevertheless, we can't trust blindly in the drawing. It could have been drawn by hands other than Mies'.

An aerial photograph of the constructed building helps dispel all doubt, however.

The few northside trees are, in fact, very distant and all but non-existent on the right, while on the west, east and south sides there are trees very close to. The drawing, then, is true to life.

We can affirm that Mies is not behind the north facade.

Mies may be in any part of the building, except to the rear of the south entrance, behind the four metal uprights of the south facade and behind the entire north facade.

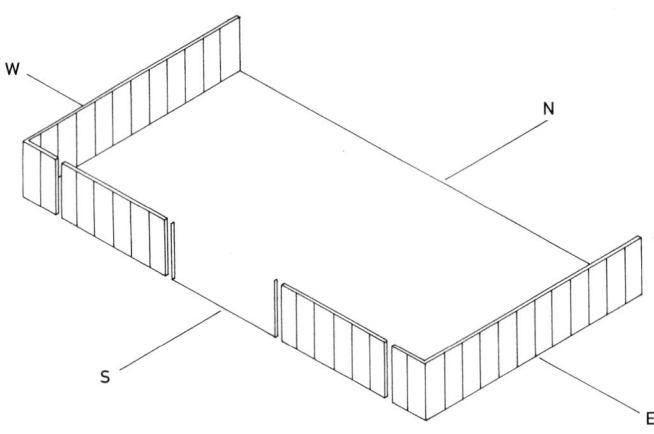

Where is Mies van der Rohe?

➜ Let's look down at the ground.
The joints of the flagstones can be made out. They appear to be rectangular, although it's possible they're square and that we think they're rectangular because of the photographic distortion.
Let's enlarge the image of the floor, using the same vanishing point as the photograph. No doubt about it, the flagstones are rectangular.

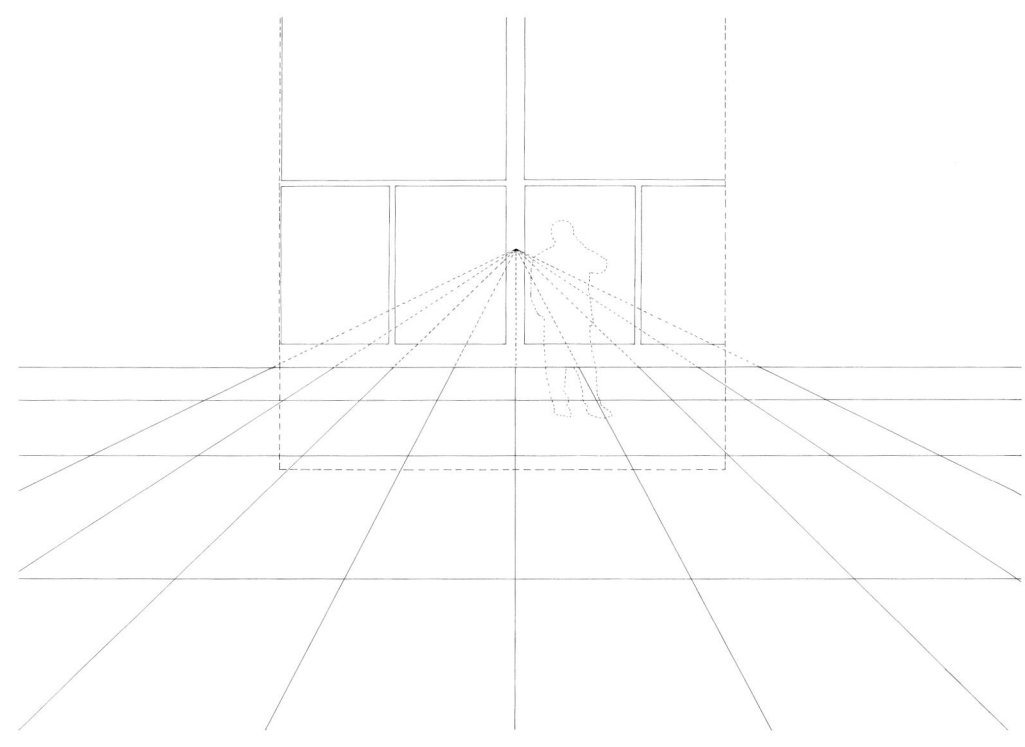

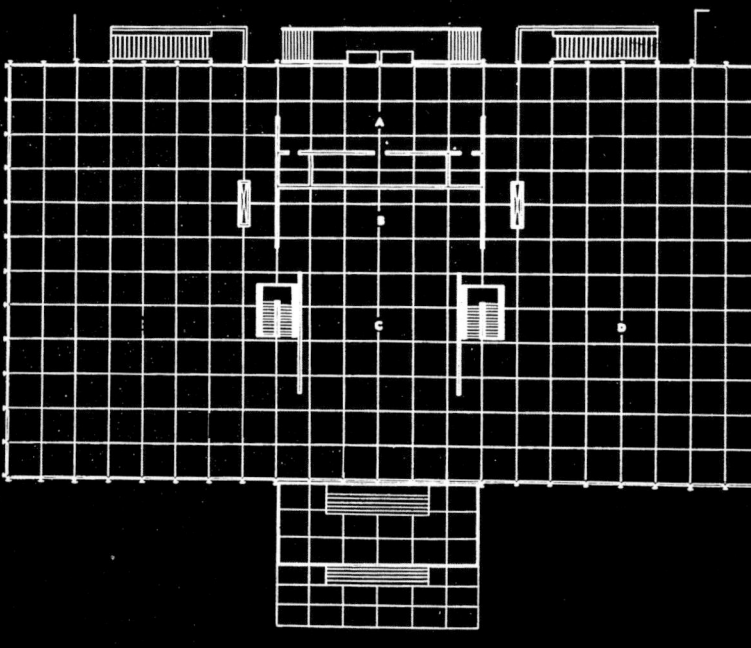

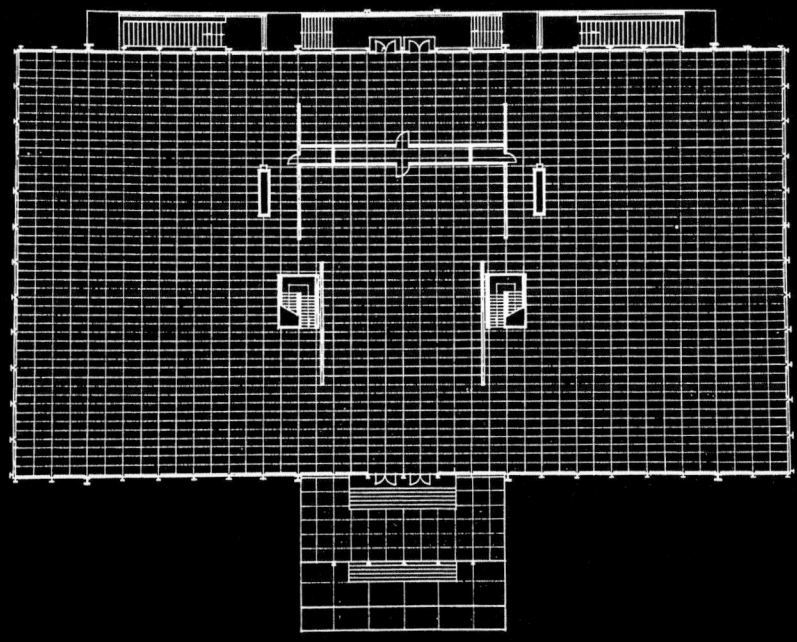

However, in some of the Crown Hall floorplan drawings the floor has been depicted with square flagstones, while in other drawings they're rectangular. What's the right shape?

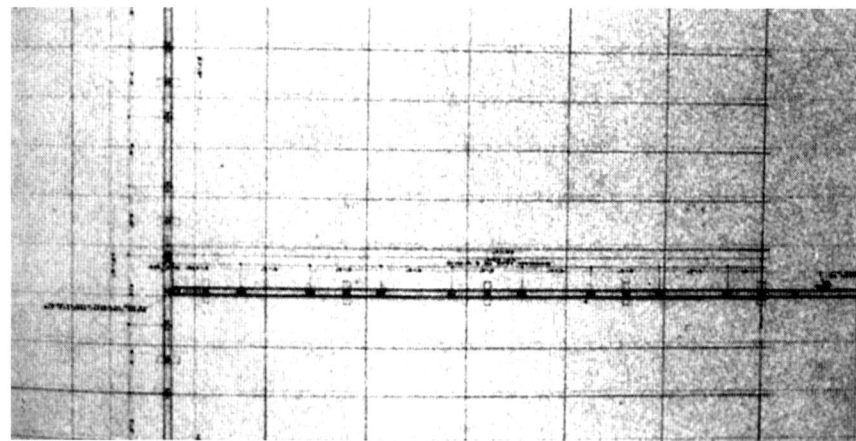

Let's check the construction details. Yes, the floor is made of rectangular flagstones, and what's more they're laid out in the same direction as the building. The dimensions of each flagstone are proportional to those of the whole building; that is, each flagstone is like a reduced Crown Hall floorplan. This means that the short sides of the flagstones are parallel and abut onto the short side of the Crown Hall building. Hence the wall in the photograph can only be one of the two short lateral walls.

Mies is, therefore, behind one of the lateral facades; that is, behind the west facade or the east facade. Mies cannot be in any other part of the building.

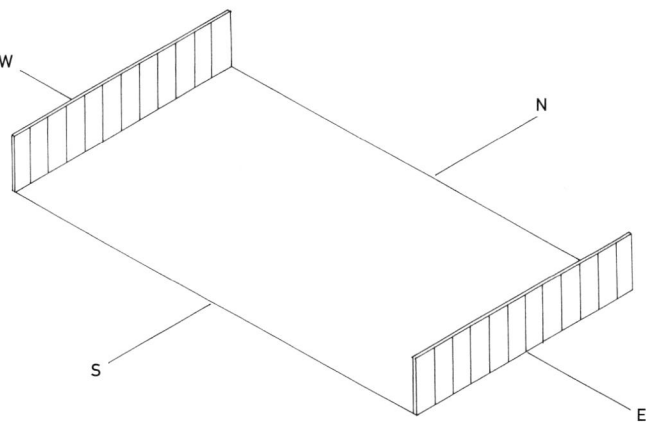

But where is Mies van der Rohe?

➜ Let's now look up at the strip of ceiling the photograph happens to include at the top.
The frame of the blinds, together with the metal upright, don't touch the ceiling; they pass behind it. This suggests that the ceiling doesn't get any support from the wall but hangs, rather, from the roof.

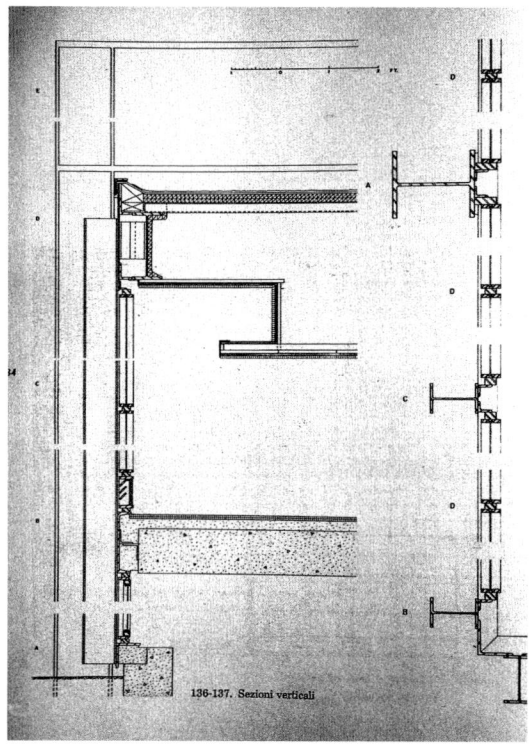

136-137. Sezioni verticali

In fact, Mies hadn't just moved the four structural colonnades outwards to free the inside space, but also to hold up the ceiling without using vertical supports. That is, the curtain wall of the facade doesn't abut onto or support the ceiling. The latter is entirely suspended.

The same Engdahl photograph, published twenty-five years later in number 124 (1981) of the Japanese magazine *A + U*, reveals a small detail missing from the first publication of the photograph.

Photo by Hedrich-Blessing

The framing of the photograph has been slightly extended towards the right, allowing us to get a glimpse of one of the corners of the suspended ceiling.

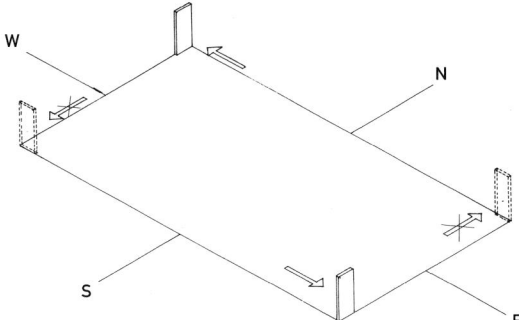

Mies, then, must be in one of the four corners. As the photograph was taken from the extreme right, and we have disregarded the north and south facades, Mies can only be in the right-hand corner of the west side or in the right-hand corner of the east side.

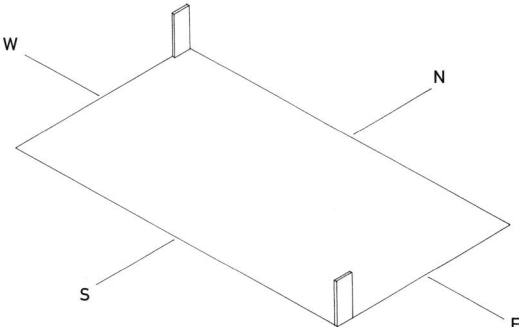

In which of the two corners is Mies van der Rohe?

→ Having got this far, one might begin to entertain the possibility of an error at the moment of printing the photograph.
What if it's been printed the wrong way round, as has often happened in magazines and books on architecture?
Like in the following dynamic sequence of three photographs of Mies, found in the book *Il design di Mies van der Rohe, Mobili e interni* edited by Werner Blaser.

Let's compare the sequence with a new photograph in which Mies appears in his apartment, next to a sculpture by Pablo Picasso and a painting by Paul Klee. All the photographs have been taken in the same place, but at different moments and from different angles.
The Paul Klee painting, common to all the photographs, confirms this.
The photograph in which the Picasso sculpture appears is published the right way round.

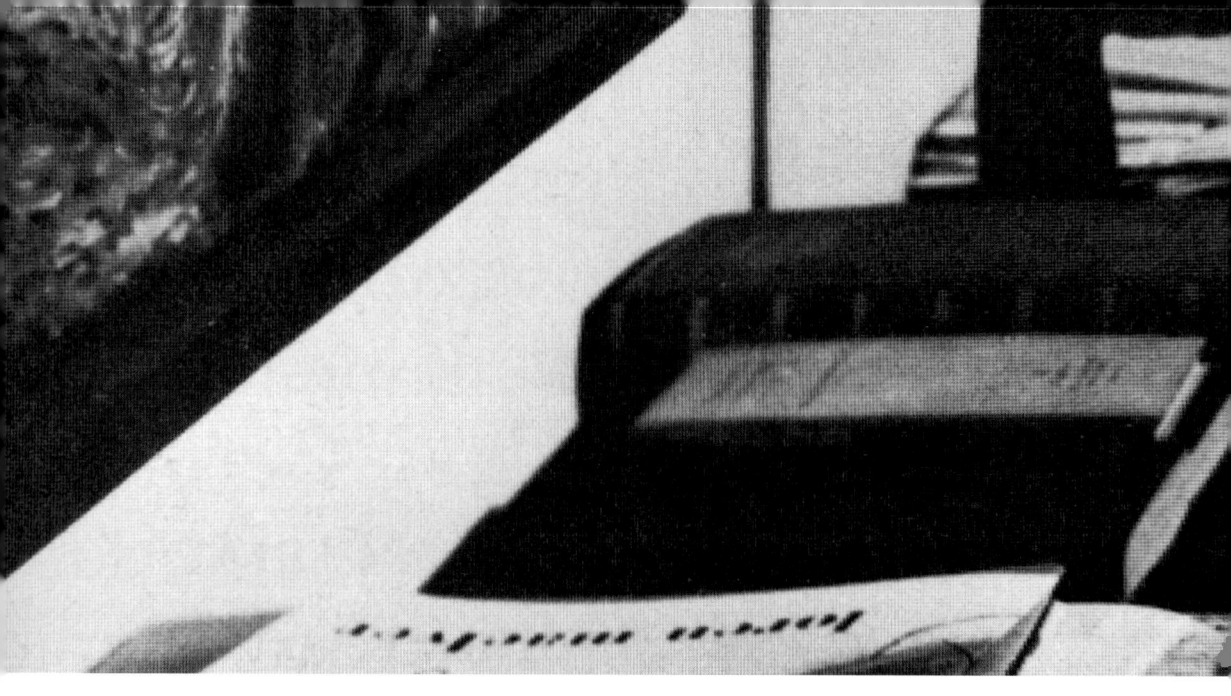

We know this from the disposition of the two words written on the white sheet of paper which the photograph happens to include at its lower left side; "loren maelver" can be read on it.
If the photograph had been the wrong way round the words would be too.

Having said that, if we compare the omnipresent Klee painting, we deduce that the one in the Werner Blaser book is the wrong way round, and thus the whole sequence of photographs too.

But, is our photograph the wrong way round? If this suspicion were well-founded, any attempt to situate Mies would come to a halt right here. Without being sure which of the two possible faces of the photographs is the right one, Mies could be anywhere, taking a step back and leaving us high and dry in any of the Crown Hall building's four corners.
The two copies of our photograph have been published twenty-five years apart, with different framing, which diverts suspicion insofar as it's highly unlikely that the same mistake has been made in different publications.

But what if the second photograph were a mechanical copy of the first, and the latter were the wrong way round?

This is unlikely, because the normal thing would be that a copied photograph would reduce, not extend, the visual field.

Let's try to figure out if our photograph is the wrong way round.

Until now we've concentrated on the materials: glass, metal and stone.

What is there left to examine?

Maybe Mies himself.

It's very difficult to find an image of Mies in which he isn't wearing an impeccable dark suit. Most of them made-to-measure by Knizé.The delicate point of a folded white handkerchief sticks out of his jacket pocket. Any person who wears a jacket, or might have simply noticed the position of the breast pocket of a jacket, knows that the pocket is on the left, never on the right. Knizé would never violate this rule, nor Mies wear something with a pocket on the right.

If the photograph were the wrong way round, the jacket would have a pocket to the right. The correct photograph, like the correct jacket, has the pocket to the left. The photograph is not the wrong way round.[2]

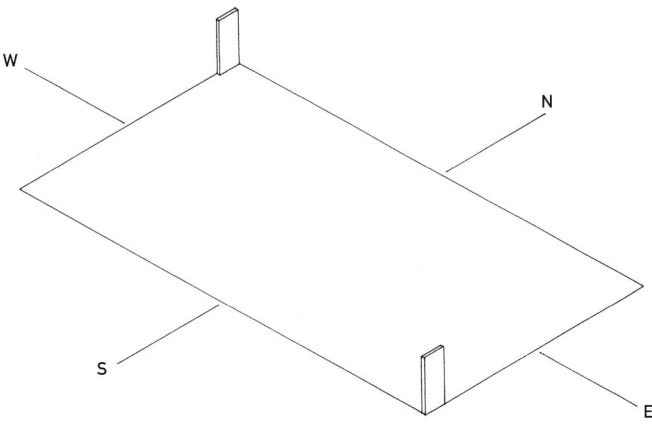

But where is Mies van der Rohe? In the right-hand corner of the west side or in the right-hand corner of the east side?

➜ Someone, distant from yet close to this investigation, made the following observation: the photograph shows us, projected on the ground, the shadow of Mies and of the metal uprights. It's said that Mies used to get up at midday and was only accustomed to working in the afternoons. Given the way the shadows fall on the floor, Mies must be in the northwest corner then. In the afternoon the sun would cast its light from the west and would produce those shadows.

The notion is encouraging but lacks credibility. The shadows on the ground can also be a product of the internal light of the building, or maybe of the feeble sunlight at any hour of the day, even the feeble light of a cloudy day – as that day seems to have been.

Those shadows wouldn't appear vertical, however, because the blinds aren't symmetrical: one is open and one is closed, and Mies is in front of the closed blinds. The light, therefore, enters from the left side, through the open blinds, and the shadows on the floor, if they are such, would appear leaning towards the right.

What we see are not shadows, but the inverted reflections of Mies and the metal uprights on the polished flagstone, which acts as a mirror.

➜ Let's go inside the Crown Hall building and take another look at its interior. Maybe there is some detail or slight movement to help us. We know that Mies cleared the interior of the building of structural elements so as to keep the whole area of the main hall free.
It could thereby be adapted to many different functions.

The main hall has, in fact, been the setting for exhibitions, formal meetings, dances and concerts without, for all that, ceasing to be a classroom or a series of spaces for classrooms, and where the actual classes of the School of Architecture, of which Mies was not only a professor but also the director, are still given today.

All the activities which required a more conventional subdividing of the space, such as the restrooms, various offices, special classrooms and the current workshops of the teaching program of the Design Institute, directed in the 50s by Jay Doblin, and then by Serge Chermayef and the Constructivist László Moholy-Nagy – with whom Mies had serious differences –, were located on the lower level of the semi-basement.[3]

From outside this level doesn't seem to exist, because it is half-buried and is ventilated and illuminated by a strip of perimetral windows which, on the outside, are the ones in contact with the level of the ground.

The main hall, however, is six feet higher than the outside ground-level and is reached by a wide staircase with travertine steps and a landing on the south side, or by two narrower symmetrical staircases on the north side.

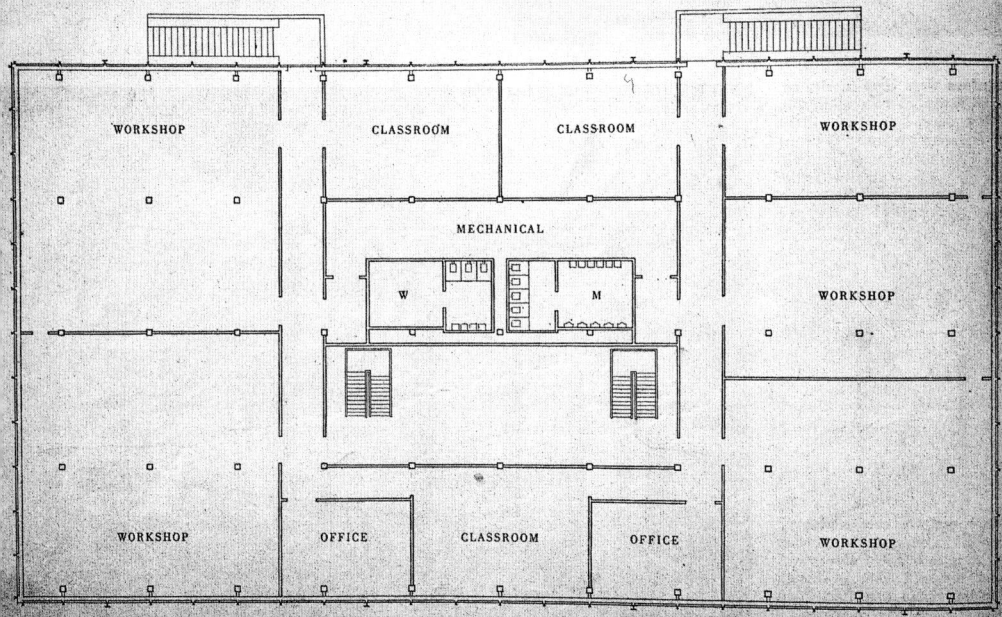

BASEMENT PLAN

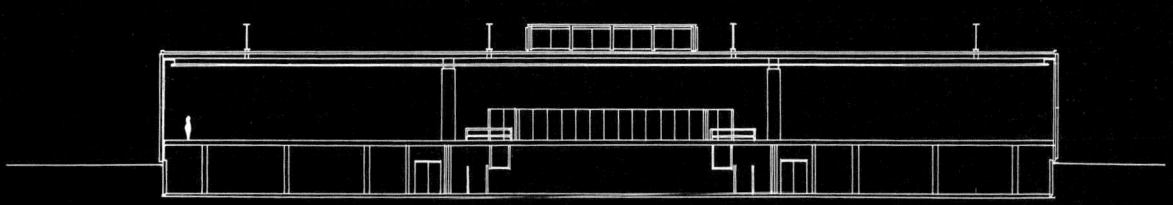

The deck which separates the hall and the basement is supported on a conventional system of reinforced-concrete pillars, with 20 x 30 foot bays which function totally independently of the metal system enclosing the upper main hall.

➜ Let's pause a moment on the flagstones of the main hall and look out from its interior.

Two students of the school of architecture appear to be working on a project. A wooden partition is visible to their back, and, behind this partition, the curtain wall. We know that the image contains one of the two possible corners in which Mies is found.

We know this, what's more, because of the hanging edge of the ceiling, the position of the flagstones and the direction of the lamps which are set into the soundproof panelling of the ceiling, parallel to the long sides of the building. The students are next to a corner, in front of a lateral wall. If we look towards the outside we can make out the hazy outline of some buildings in the distance. And the tree?

In the photograph with Mies in it there's a tree very close to the facade. In this new image there are a number of trees, but they don't coincide with the one in the photograph of Mies.

Our tree is to be found behind the second module going from right to left. In the new image, there's no tree behind this second module.

Mies cannot be in the corner where the students are, because there's no tree there. Necessarily, Mies has to be in the opposite corner.

If we find out which corner the students are in, we will automatically know what corner Mies is in. Let's step back a bit from the students.

Mies placed a series of natural oak partitions in the main hall, some of them fixed, which defined the exhibition areas, together with the administration office and a small bookstore. Others were removable and used as needed. The partitions enabled secluded work areas to be created, but they didn't drastically subdivide the main hall. Their height is no more than 8 feet, in contrast to the 18 feet of the hall.

Let's step back still further from the students. Aside from the partitions, the photograph shows us the metal handrails of the stairs linking the main hall level to the lower, semi-basement level, and two large pilasters which appear to be structural, but are not: they contain the full-height installation cores extending from the illuminated ceiling to the reflecting floor.[4]

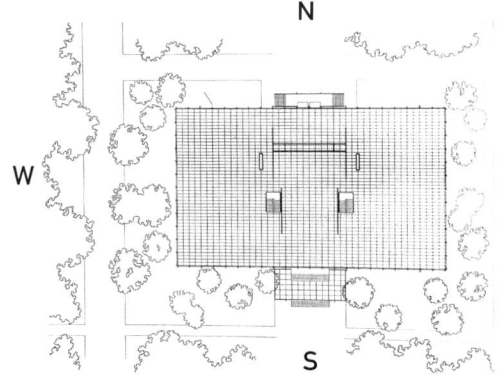

Both the installation cores and the interior staircases, plus the partitions for fixed exhibitions, have been placed symmetrically by Mies in relation to the north-south axis, though not in relation to the east-west one. The Crown Hall building is not symmetrical with respect to the east-west axis.

In order, in the image with the students, for the pilasters to be seen to the left of the stairs the photograph has to have been taken from the southwest corner. This indicates that the corner in the image is the southeast one. And, if there is no tree in that corner, then Mies cannot be there.

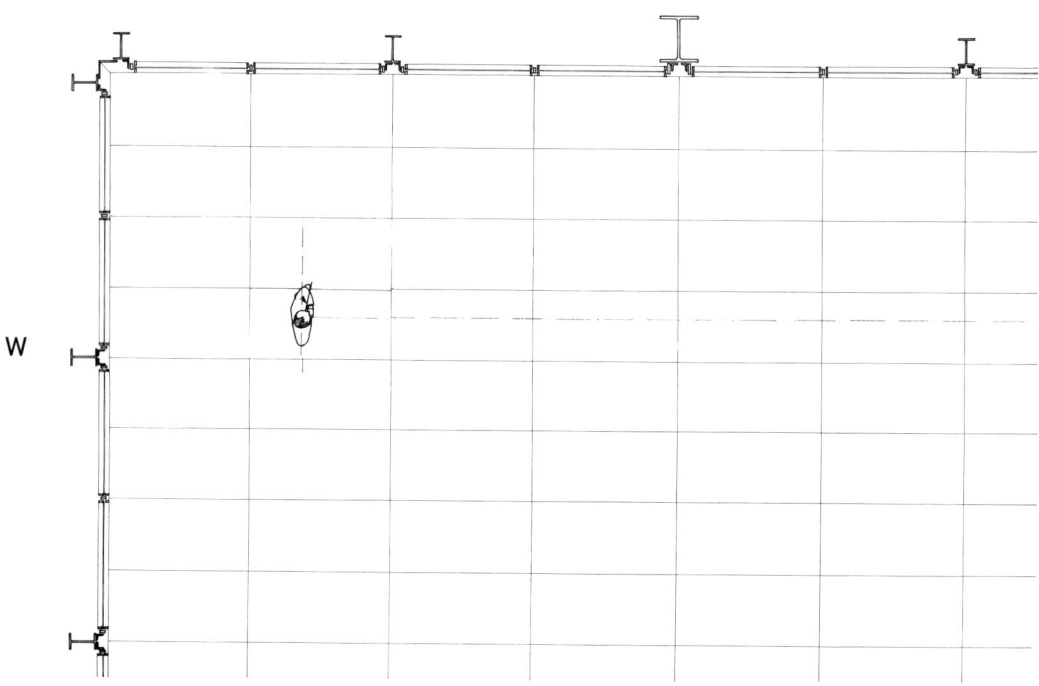

N

W

Mies and the tree can only be in the opposite corner, the northwest one. There's no other possibility. Mies is in the northwest corner of the Crown Hall building, with his back 6.74 feet from the west side and 7.75 feet to the right of the north side, in the interior of the main hall.

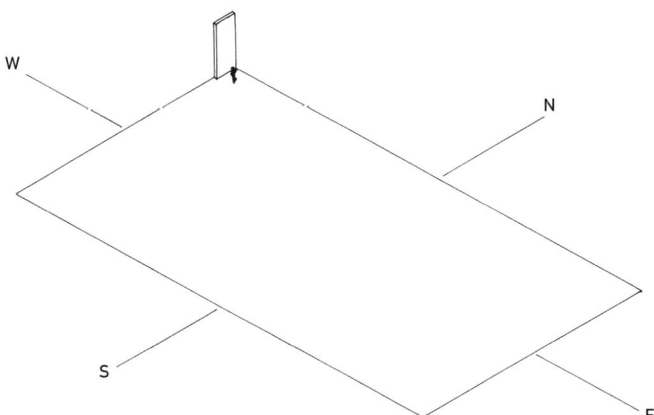

Who would ever have imagined that Mies himself had left the faint pencil drawing of that corner of the building, with firstly the tree and a shadowy figure, perhaps the memory or prophecy of himself entering the building on that overcast afternoon?

He's got out of the car, there he is, approaching the north corner of the building. Now he slowly mounts the stairs. His legs hurt. He stops to rest. He enters. Engdahl has been waiting some time for him. They speak, point, discuss, finally reach agreement. He's drawn towards that corner. He stops, turns, adjusts his pocket handkerchief, changes his cigar to the other hand, puffs on it, observes, shifts his balance onto one leg, puts his hand in his pocket, fixes his gaze. Looks. Waits.
Outside, the Acacia, ever watchful, waits for him, listens for the click! and stretches forth its branches.

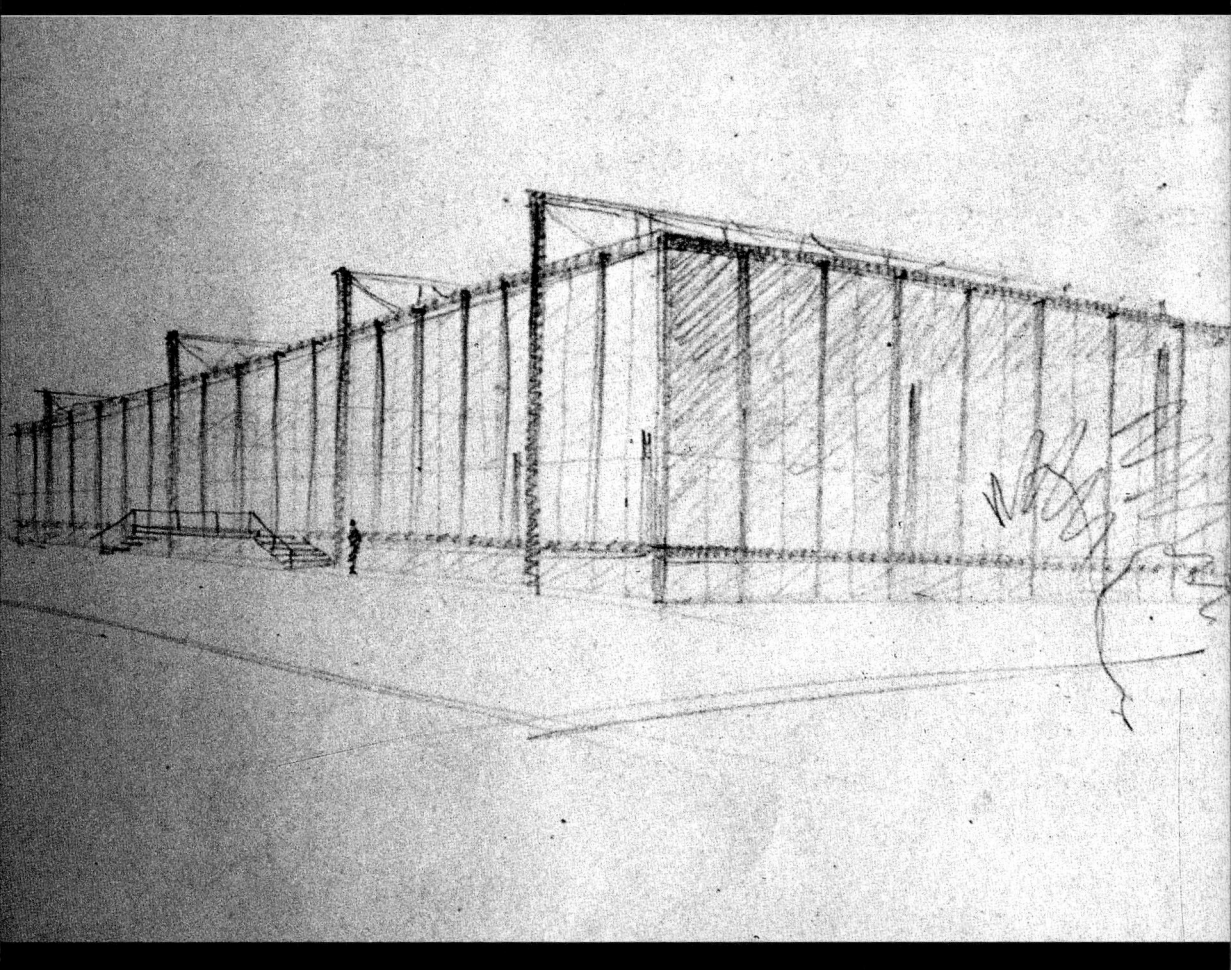

But what is Mies van der Rohe looking at?

Let's suppose that Mies could have chosen his position for some precise motive, and that the photograph is not as casual as it appears. Maybe there was an agreement with the photographer, not only to choose the place but to assume a precise and definite pose as well.
Why is Mies in that particular spot?
What is Mies van der Rohe looking at?

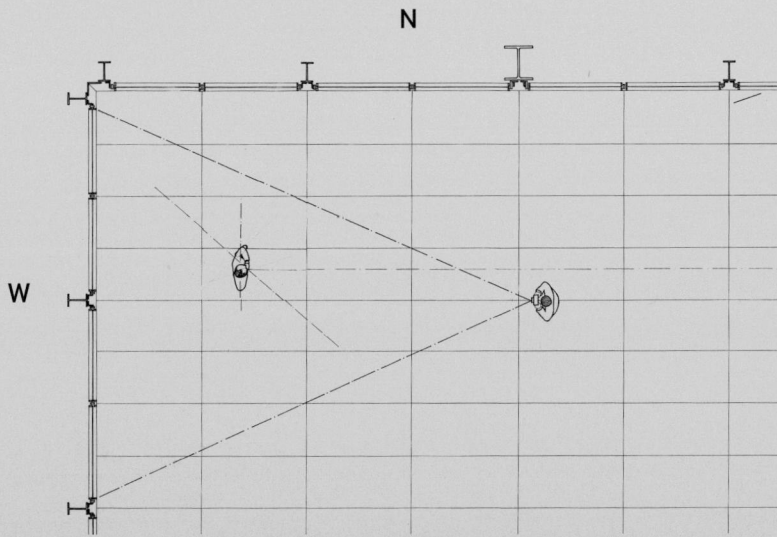

→ Engdahl, in fact, placed the camera right on one of the joints of the paving, making it coincide with the axis of the metal upright, at a distance of 13.11 feet from Mies and 10 feet from the north side.

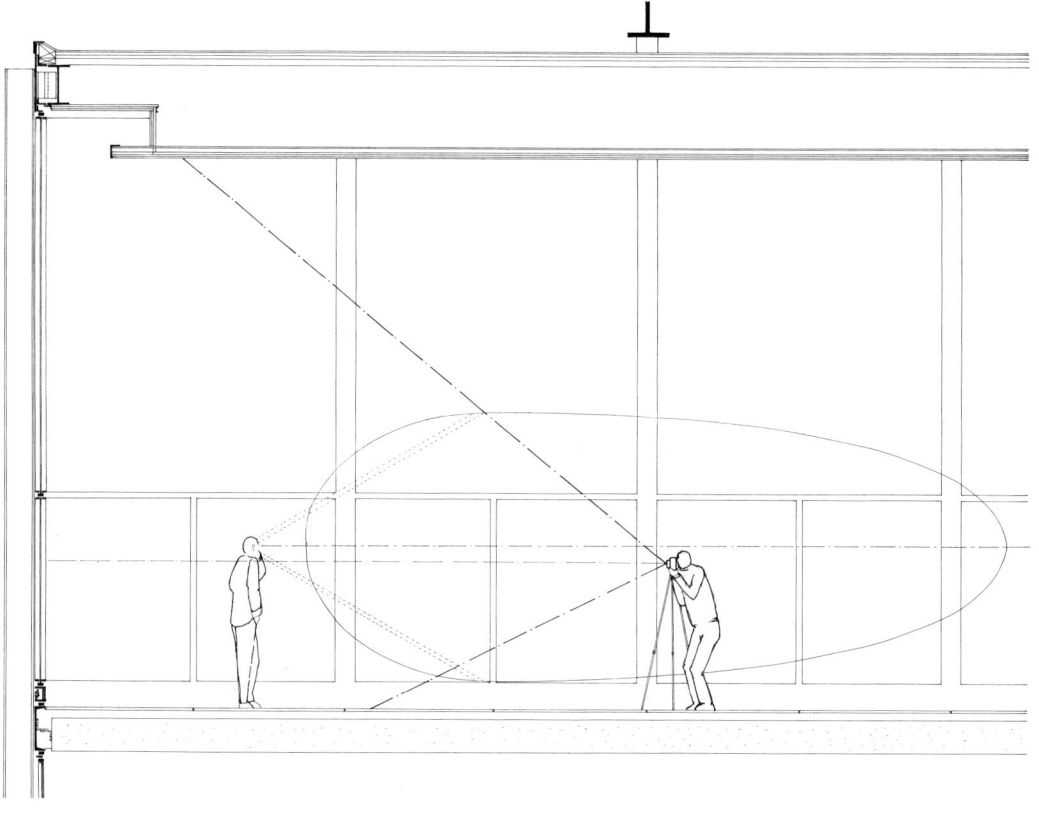

Mies' eyes are slightly off-center in relation to the axis of the lens:
6 inches above and 18 inches to the right of the axis of the lens.
This was doubtless the best composition for the photograph.

In a first setup Engdahl could have had the center of the lens coincide with the center of Mies' head, but, given his position and the distance between both, the background would be decentered and the framing would exclude the branches of the tree. The Acacia was necessary.

But there's more: no matter what might have been behind it, the right-hand blind was closed intentionally and Mies positioned himself or moved 18 inches to the right of the central joint in order to avoid coinciding with the center of the lens.

In Engdahl's view, Mies could neither position himself in front of the metal upright, cutting it off and having it grow out of the middle of his head, or to the left, unbalancing the framing and competing with the Acacia.
There was no other spot for Mies.

The framing was a perfect, calculated balance of opposites.
To the left, the blurred branches of the tree, the open blinds, the light.
To the right, Mies in his black suit, the closed blinds, the darkness.
But it wasn't just the position; Mies chose a particular pose as well.

→ It's common, in images of Mies, to see him smoking – the chosen photograph is no exception. A cigar goes along with his distant gaze. If the cigar seems to have no importance, let's take a look at some other images of him smoking.

They seem to merely confirm the habit, but there's one detail common to all. Mies holds the cigar in his right hand. This could mean several things; firstly, we might care to speculate on his right-handedness.

Let's look at the image of Mies together with his brother Ewald.
In it the cigar hanging from his mouth has still not been lit.

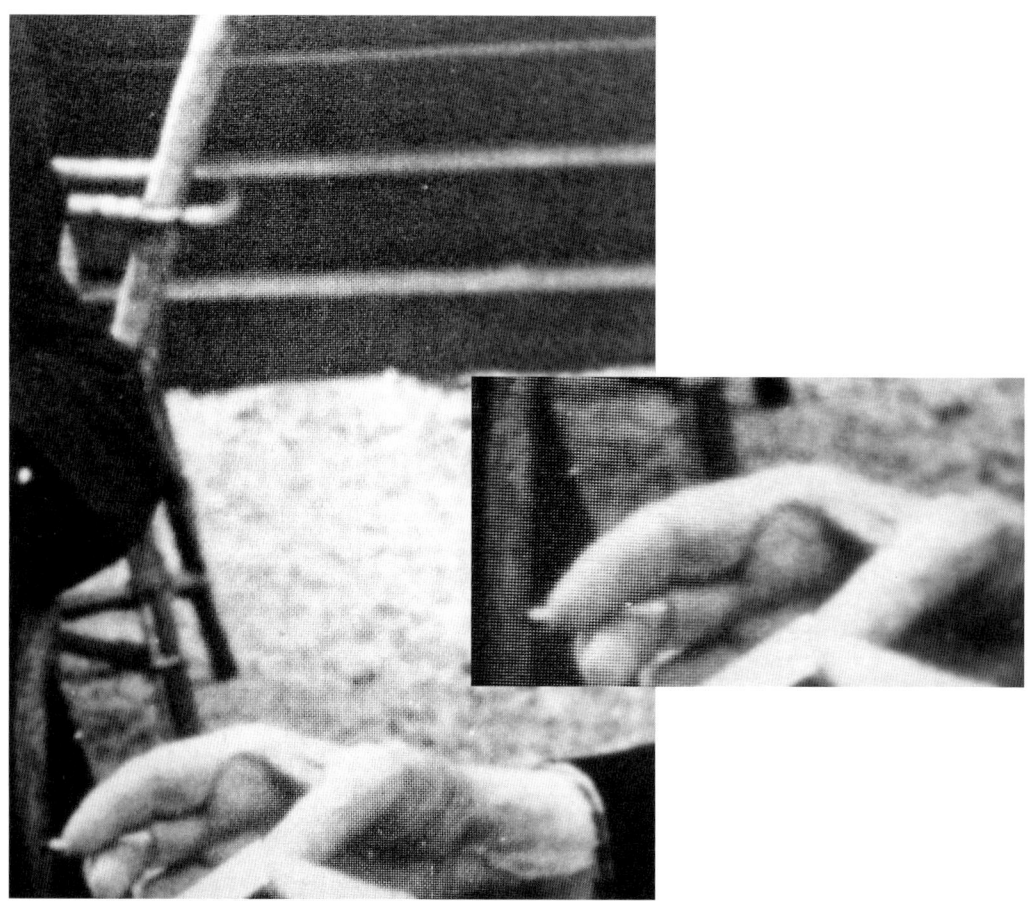

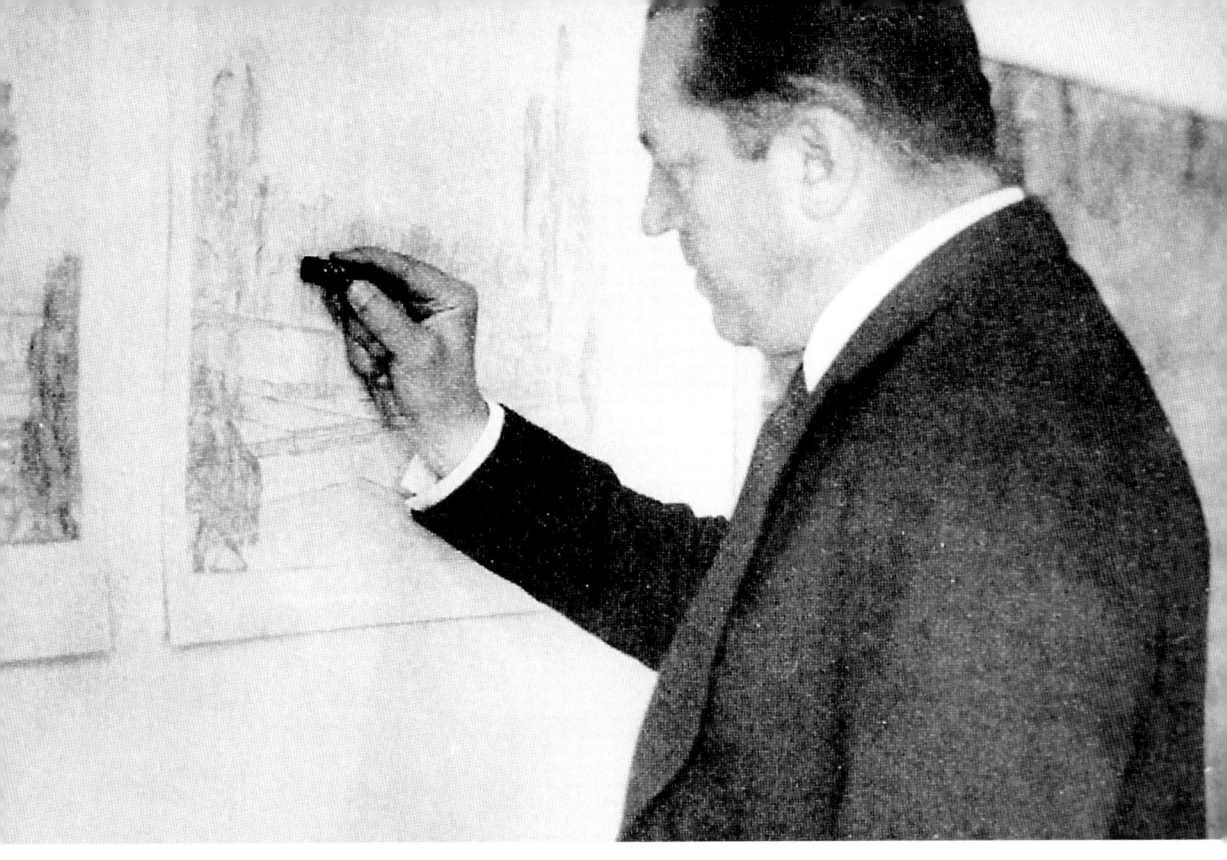

If we get nearer his hands, we see that in one of them there's a match awaiting the friction that will turn it into flame.
Which hand does Mies hold the match in? Once more in the right; added to which he also draws with that hand.

If Mies usually holds the cigar in his right hand, why in the chosen photograph is he holding it in his left? We've already rejected the possibility that the photograph is the wrong way round...

Perhaps Mies changed the cigar to his other hand intentionally. It's possible that Mies, in cooperation with Engdahl, decided on a particular pose for the photo. It shouldn't surprise us that Mies and his photographers organized any image of him down to the last detail.

→ It suffices to compare the next two photographs.
Mies, seated on one of his tubular steel chairs, the 1926 MR10, seems to be holding an animated conversation with an unseen interlocutor.
The photos have, without a doubt, been taken in a single place and on a single occasion: the table, the ashtray, the rug and the collages of his old friend Kurt Schwitters on the wall all confirm this. The setting is his apartment at 200 East Pearson Street in Chicago.

Only Mies' gestures, taken instants apart, seemingly differentiate one photo from the other. Even the reflections in the glass of the pictures are identical in both photographs. Yet the setting has been carefully checked and rearranged for the second photograph. Impeccable as always, Mies couldn't put up with bothersome details. The photographer, or Mies, was obliged to take note and opted to remove these.

The electrical socket on the wall, which can be seen beneath the table, the black box behind the chair and the inconvenient thread hanging from the edge of the chair – invisible to the eyes of the seated Mies, but obvious and tiresome in the eyes of the photographer, or in Mies' eyes when scrutinizing the photograph – were meticulously suppressed.

In a short space of time the scene was corrected. Perhaps the only thing missing was to eliminate the box of matches which appears to timidly hide itself from the eyes of the photographer and which finally remains as a silent witness to the rigorous clean-up or as an alibi for the improvized naturalness of the scene.

Mies himself, conscious of the subterfuge, changes his comfortable and relaxed pose; obliged to by the chair, he straightens up, adjusts his elegant jacket, puts his feet together and, to our surprise, changes his Montecristo cigar from one hand to the other: he shifts it from his right to his left hand, in the same way we assume he'd done in the Crown Hall photograph.

→ Although Mies always appears in photographs
drawing or lighting cigars with his right hand,
he doesn't always hold them in it.
Let's see the following images.

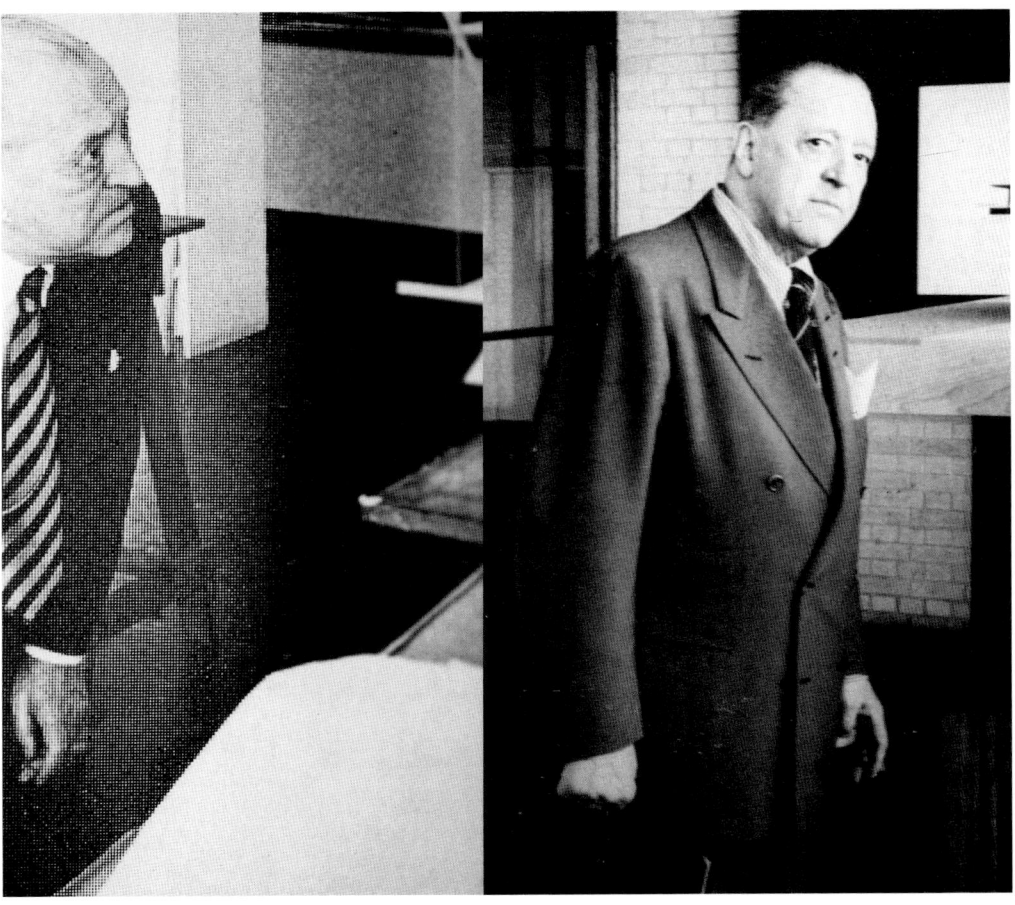

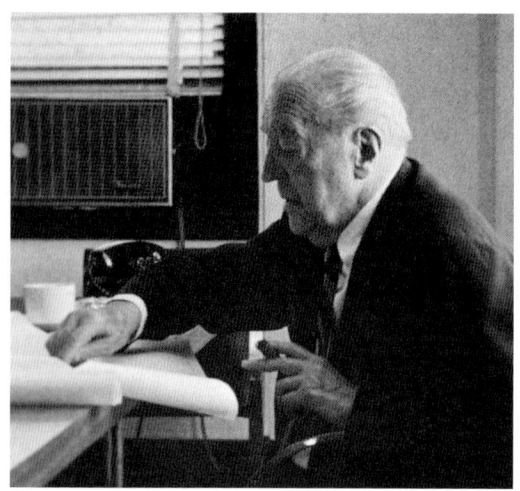

In these he holds the cigar in his left hand. That is, Mies changes his cigar indiscriminately from one hand to the other.

In fact Franz Schulze, in his *Critical Biography* of Mies, in the chapter devoted to his youth in Aachen, and describing the affinities between Mies and his older brother Ewald, writes: "The links the two brothers shared included common abilities; both were ambidextrous and had equally acute eyesight."[5] Mies indiscriminately shifts the cigar from hand to hand because he is ambidextrous. And it's highly likely that in our photograph he has changed hands, conscious of the situation.

We can verify this in the next images, taken by Engdahl inside the Crown Hall building in 1956.

The photographs most probably were taken on the same day and during the same session as ours.[6] We know this for a series of reasons. We see the 70-year-old Mies, the same lines on his expansive face – despite it being the opposite side –, same gaze, same dark suit, same creases in his white shirt, same black tie, same folded white handkerchief, same photographer, same building, and same cigar.

Yet with one difference: now he's holding it in his right hand.

Yes, no doubt about it, Mies changed his Montecristo cigar from one hand to the other. Given all this, I only want to emphasize the non-casual nature of the photograph; that is, the fact that Mies chose a particular pose, and maybe a particular location in the building, to take his position up in. Why did he choose that particular corner?

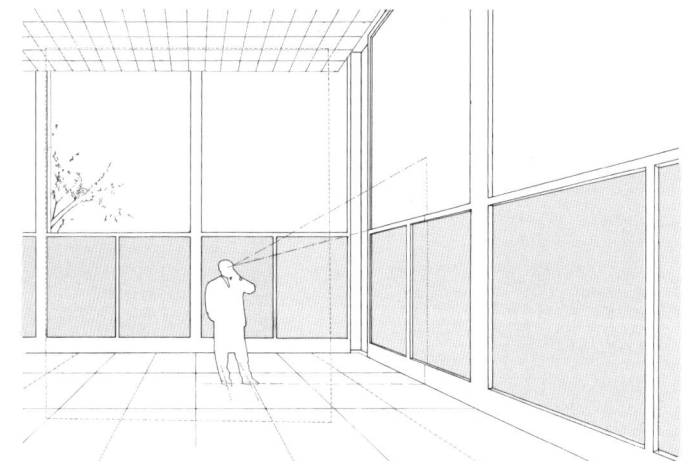

If Mies is in a corner, not only is he near the wall we see behind him, to which he has his back, but also near the one to his left, that is, the wall we do not see, which is to the right of anyone looking at the photograph. That is, Mies is not looking towards the interior of his own building, he's not gazing absent-mindedly at the main hall, as we might have supposed when looking at the photograph.

Standing hard up against the north facade, Mies is looking towards the outside of the Crown Hall building.

Is it possible that Mies positioned himself just there because it was where he could see something in particular from, something which is outside the Crown Hall building? What is Mies van der Rohe looking at?

Let's get closer to the University Campus.

115

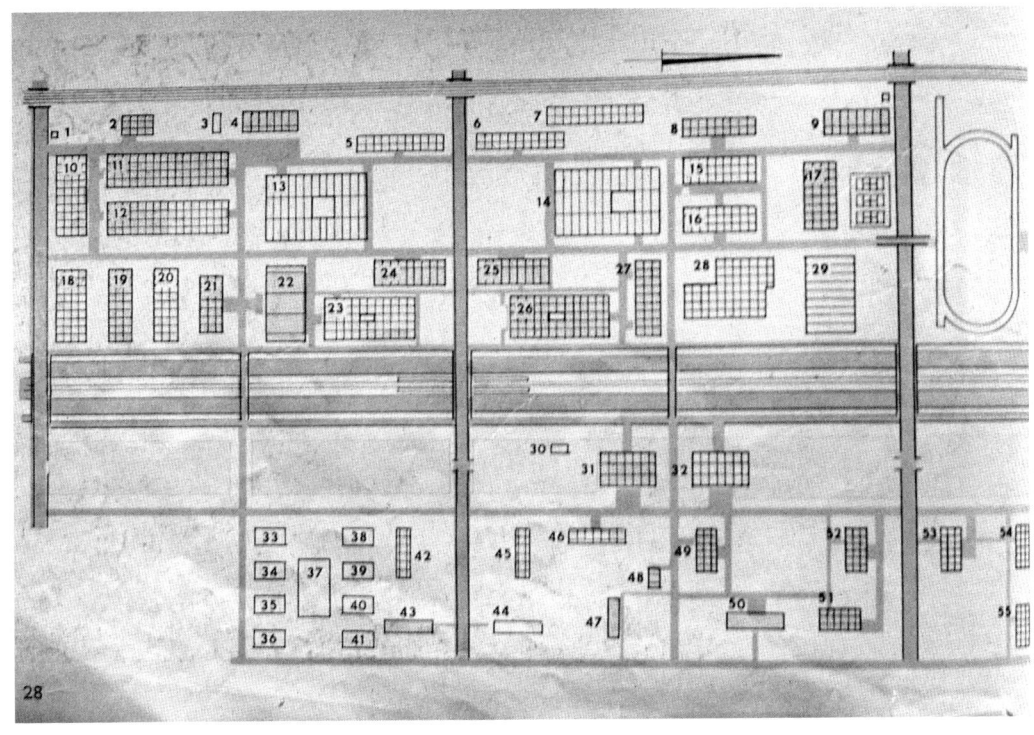

28

During that period of time the planning of the campus went through continuous changes. During one of the final stages, to all intents and purposes the last, Mies laid out, over the extensive site located on the South Side of Chicago and intended for the Institute, more than fifty buildings, not all of which, as we know, got built.

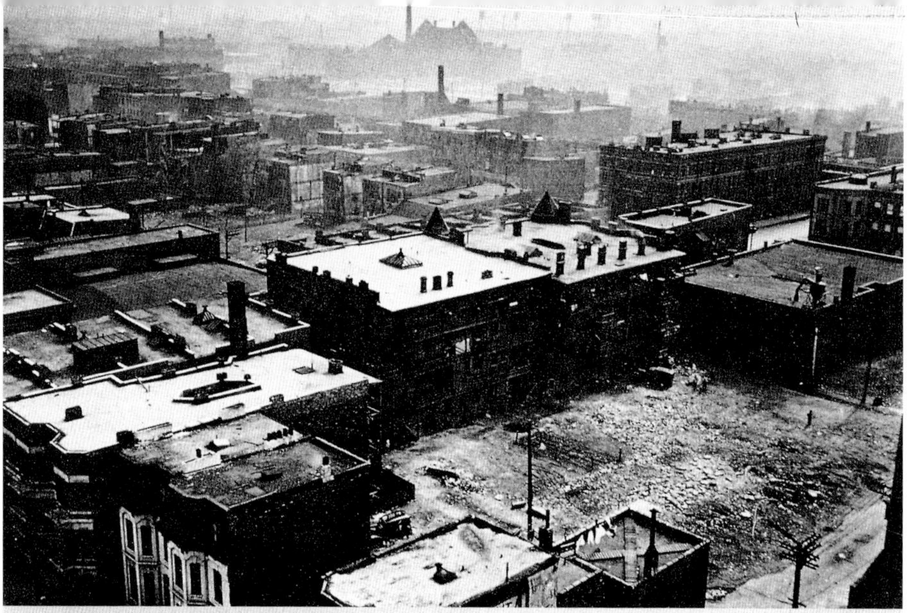

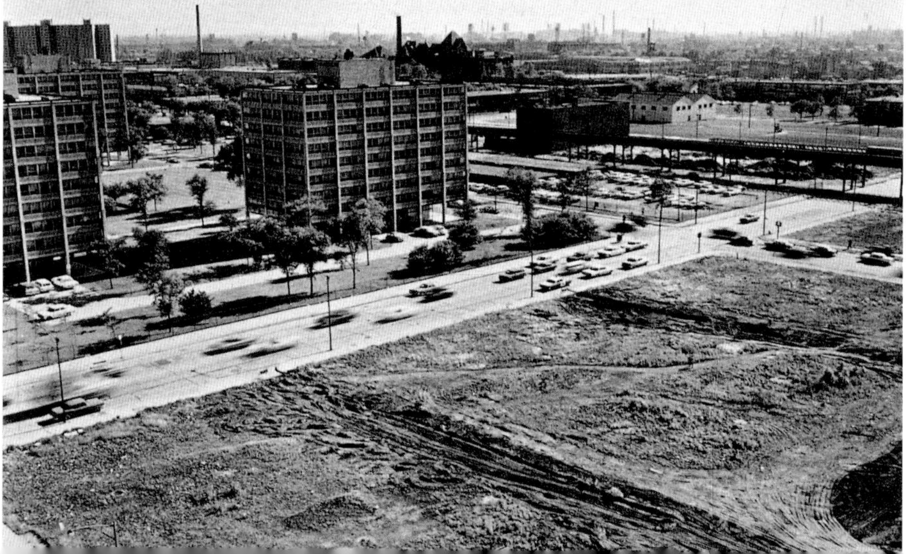

In 1958, shortly after Mies' retirement from the Institute, the IIT administration withdrew the campus commission and entrusted it to Skidmore, Owings & Merrill, the practice that had profited the most from Mies' teachings and which would vainly attempt to repeat the master's schemes in more than one of its subsequent interventions.

Let's get nearer the north side of the Crown Hall building. An aerial view helps us ascertain what there is on that side of the building. Mies sited various buildings there. The nearest one is the IIT Electrical Engineering and Physics building. It is narrower and slimmer than the Crown Hall building, but both coincide in their length, 240 feet, and in the way they make contact with the ground.

In both there is a slight change of elevation between the inside and outside levels. They appear to emerge or rise from the ground.

The IIT Electrical Engineering and Physics building is practically twice the height of the Crown Hall building. It is possible that from where he is Mies could see the Engineering building.

However, there is something about his gaze that makes this doubtful.

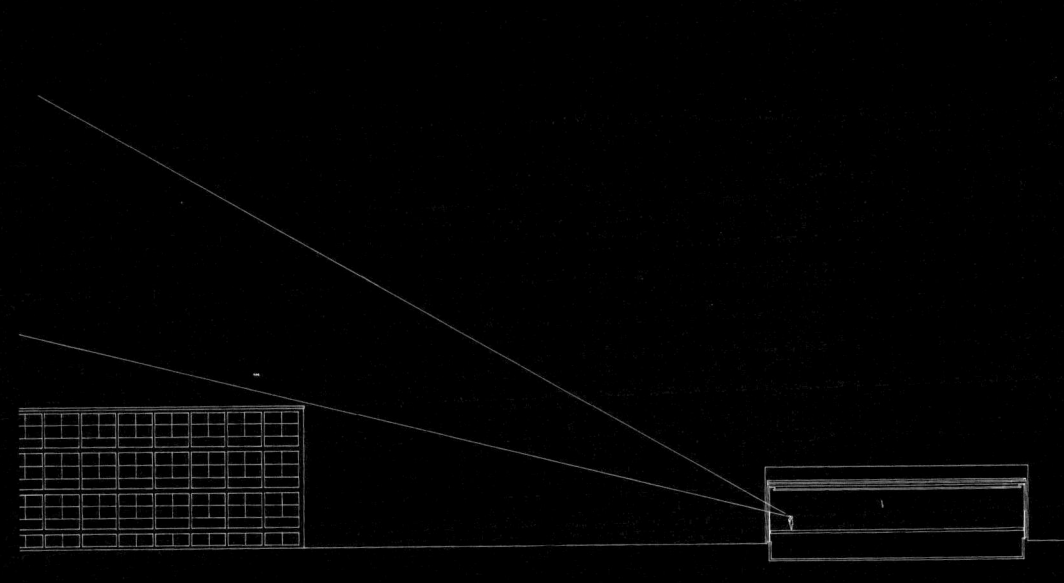

The distance between the two buildings is considerable, some 214 feet.
Let's draw the two buildings to scale.
Let's plot Mies' precise angle of vision, above the strip of frosted glass.
The lowest vector of his gaze passes above the Engineering building,
brushing against it.
Mies is not looking at it, because from his position he cannot see it.
The Engineering building is completely hidden by the frosted glass.

What is Mies van der Rohe looking at?

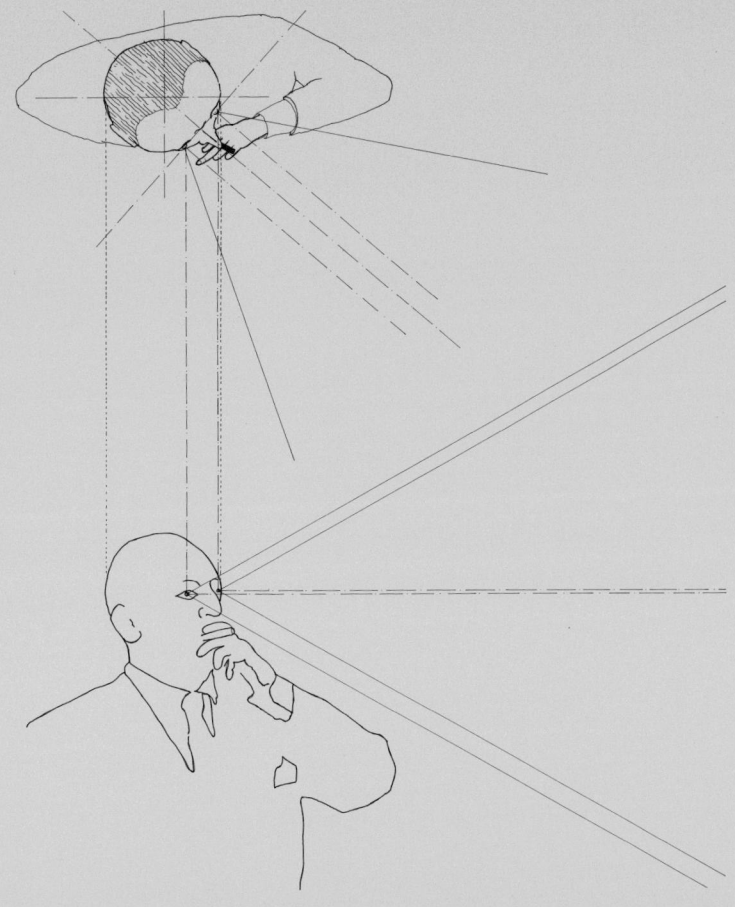

→ Let's get a bit nearer Mies. His head is slightly turned to the left in relation to his body.

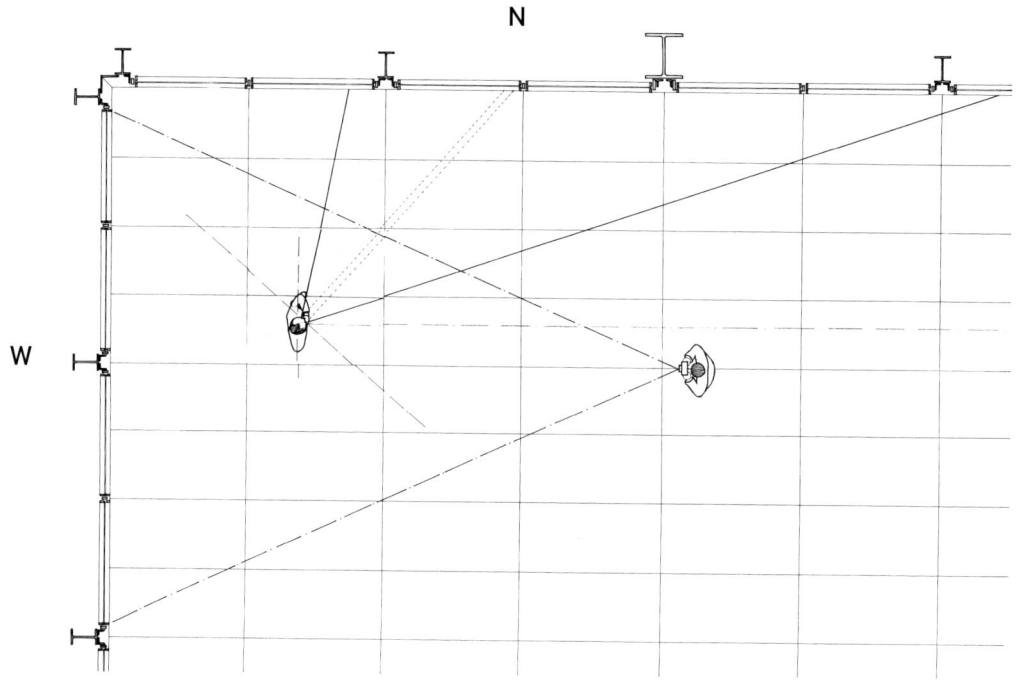

Mies is not looking straight ahead towards the north facade. His cone of vision hits the glass wall at an angle. What is he looking at, then?
If the greater part of his vision is arrested by the strip of frosted glass...

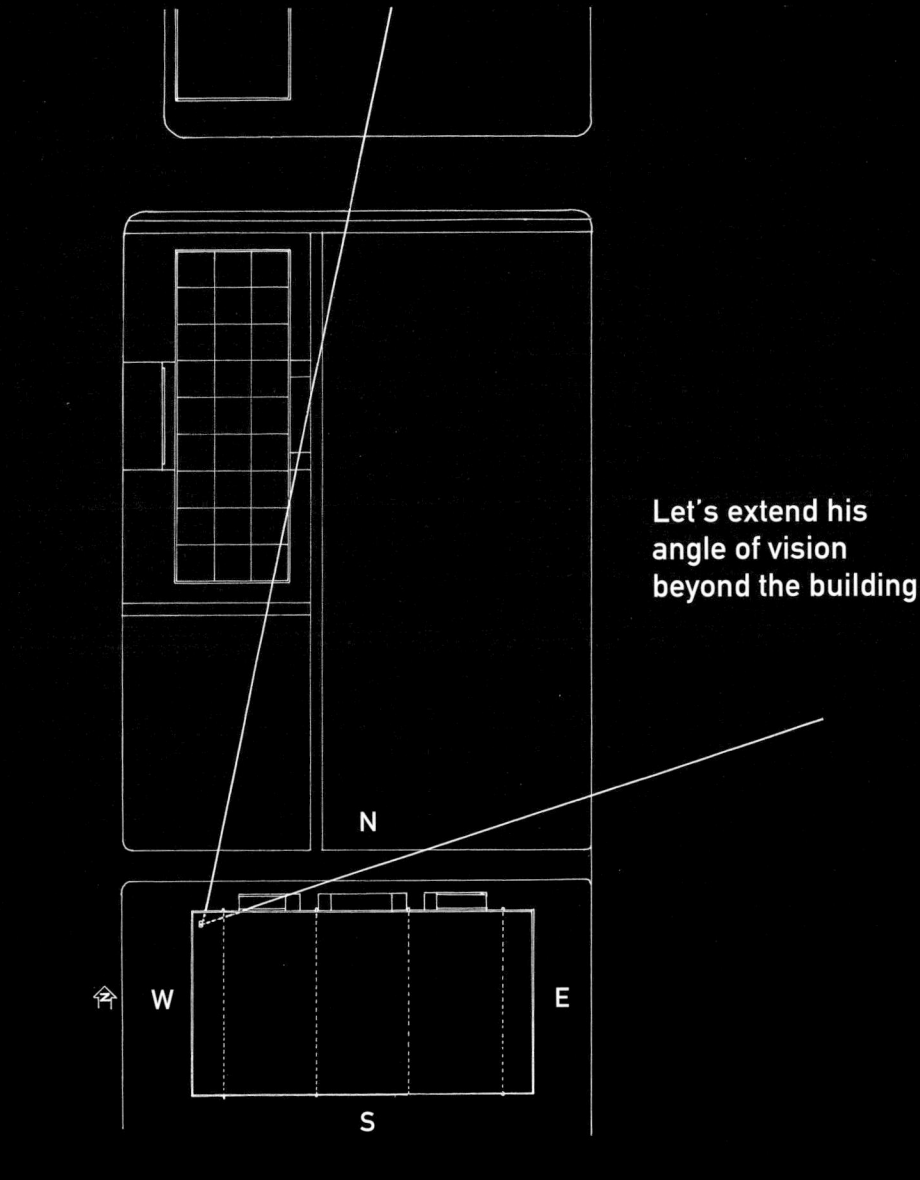

Let's extend his
angle of vision
beyond the building.

Where he seems to be looking there's nothing.

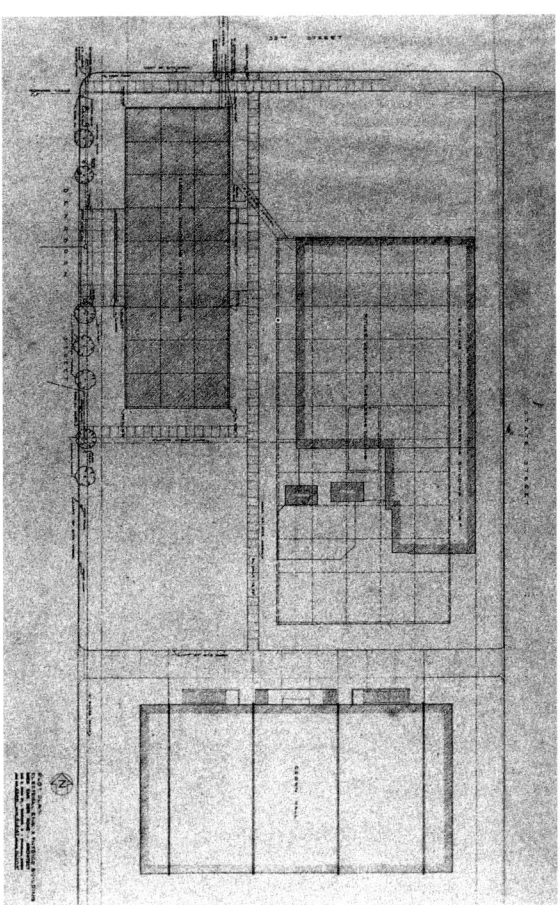

Let's go back to the original plans of the Institute.

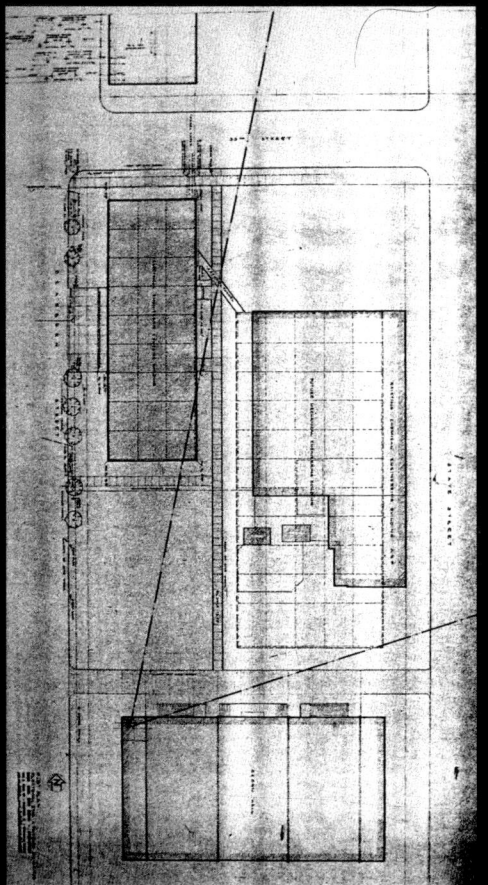

An odd building occupies that
spot. Its L-shaped form
doesn't seem to have anything
Miesian about it.
Apart from the Gymnasium,
the other Institute buildings
are all rectangular.
But this odd building just fits
into his angle of vision.
In the drawing, a stippled
rectangular shape is super-
imposed on it.

Let's get a bit nearer the image drawn on 4 September 1957 and read the inscriptions: The L-shaped image, the existent Chemical Engineering building, and the stippled building, the future Mechanical Engineering building.

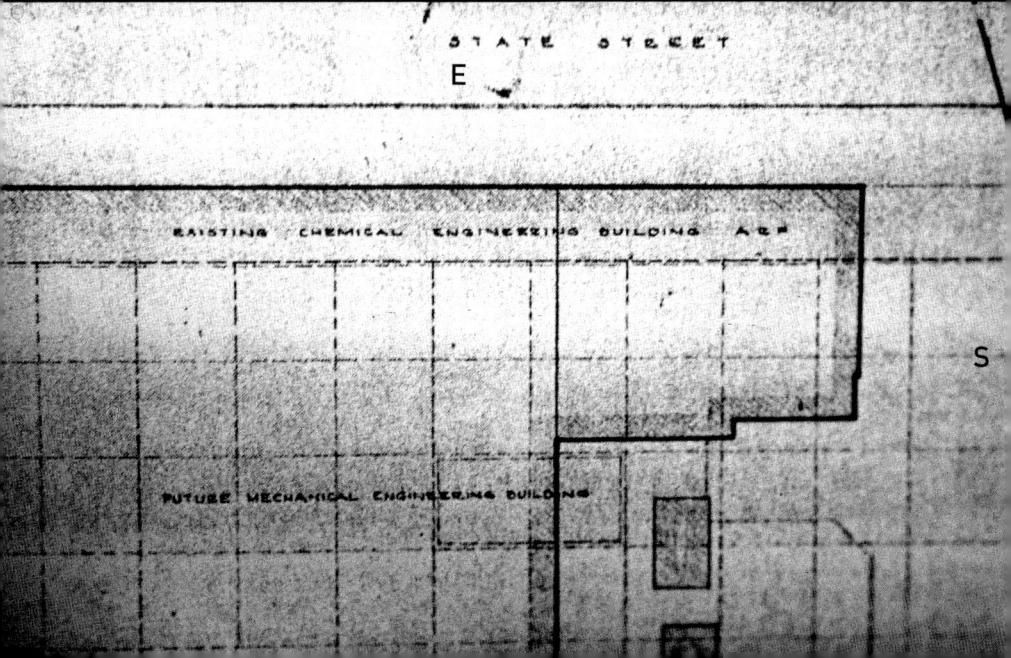

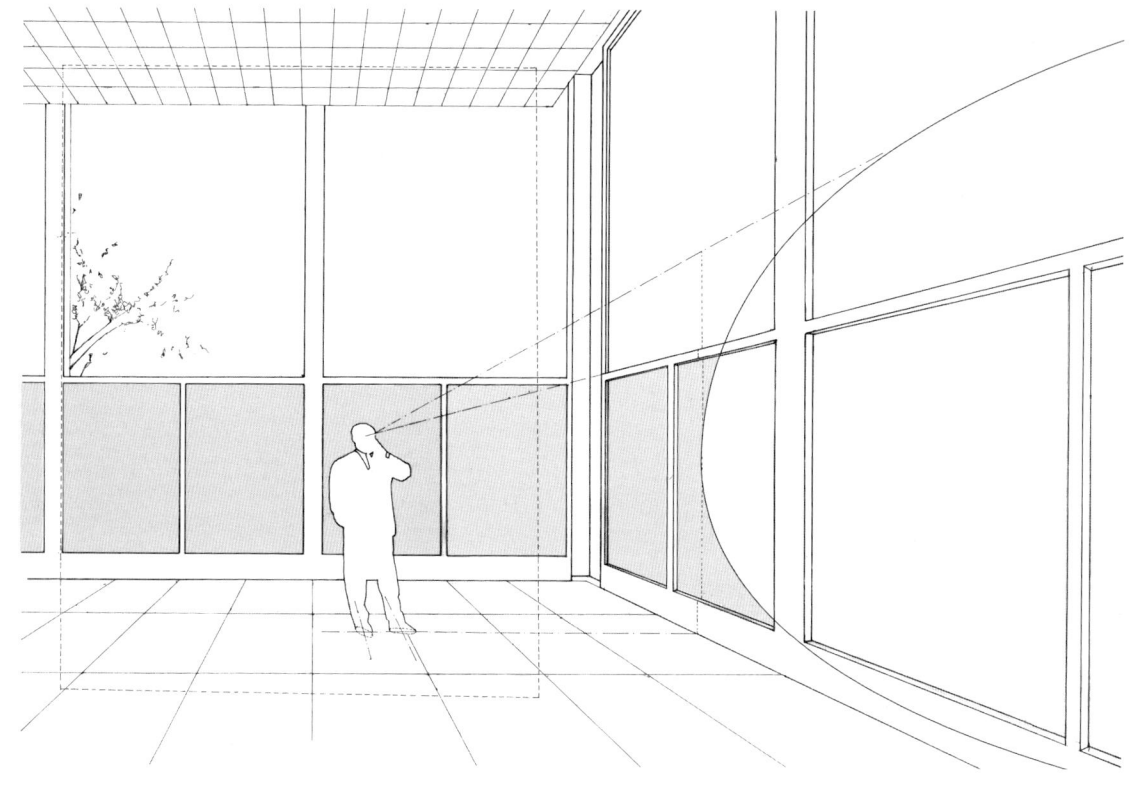

No, there's no reason for Mies' gaze being detained by the frosted glass strip:

Maybe he's imagining the Mechanical Engineering building he'd never get to build.

What is Mies van der Rohe looking at?

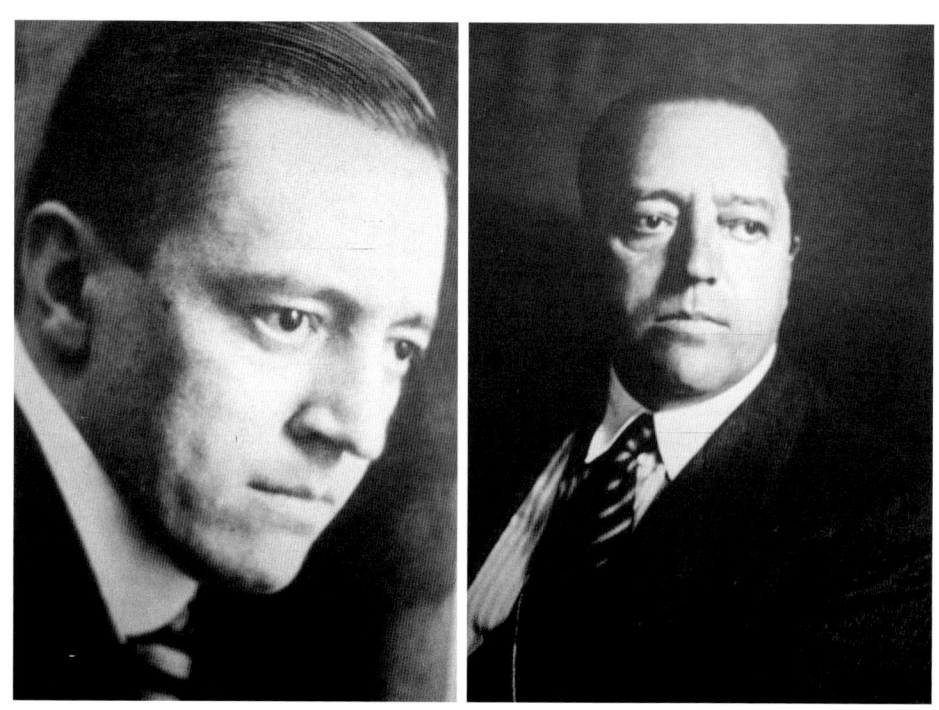

→ Let's get even nearer Mies. We already know of his excellent eyesight, praised by several generations of architecture historians. Curiously, at one time in his life he wore a monocle, something which perhaps helped accentuate his disturbing countenance. A brief and imprudent time, in the words of Schulze.

Let's get nearer his face.

Mies' eyes squint.

Photographs of his parents, Michael Mies and Amalia Rohe,[7] suggest that he could have inherited this trait from them.

Despite his excellent vision as a young man, Mies was diagnosed in his 60s as having a strabismus, accompanied by an opaque spotting of the cornea, a condition more known as leucoma,[8] that delightfully named but terrible infirmity that Joyce and Homer also suffered from: "The grayish eyes of Athena's owl," as Joyce would write, referring to Homer.

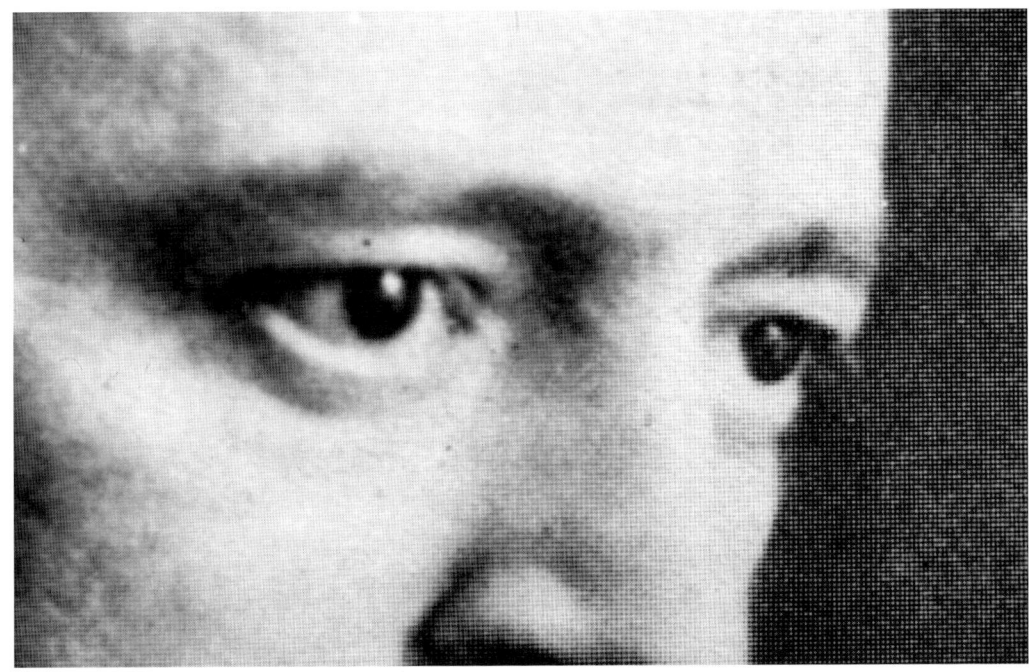

The most appropriate optical remedy consists in the use of spectacles, a palliative solution aimed only at combatting the complications involved. There's no way of treating the strabismus itself. It is a progressive and irreversible condition. Yet in none of the images we've seen up to now does Mies wear spectacles. For many years they were probably unnecessary, or maybe, unlike the monocle, they got in the way of his face. By the end of his 50s he needed them all the time.

Let's look at the photograph taken by Frank Scherschel in 1957, and not by Bill Engdahl who, as we saw, was accustomed to revising and correcting his photographs. In the image Mies has been taken unawares by Scherschel in his Chicago studio. Faced with the speed of the photograph, Mies takes off his glasses and vainly tries to keep them out of shot.

Maybe it wasn't just affectation, but the wish to present the image of himself he knew to be authentic, that drove Mies to conceal his glasses.

➜ Let's get nearer his misty hazel eyes. The person who wears spectacles withdraws from the world. He lives and perceives in the scarred and
restricted space stretching from lens to retina.

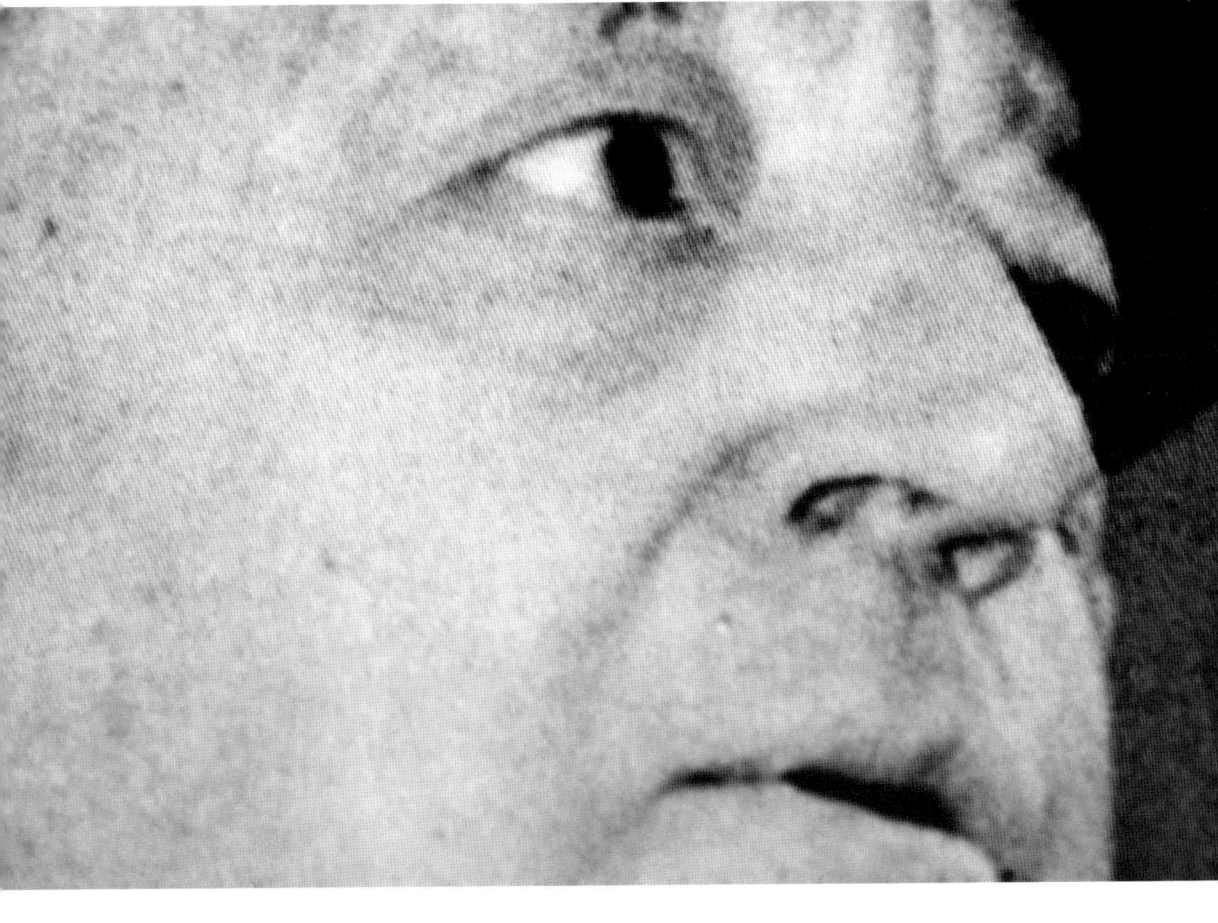

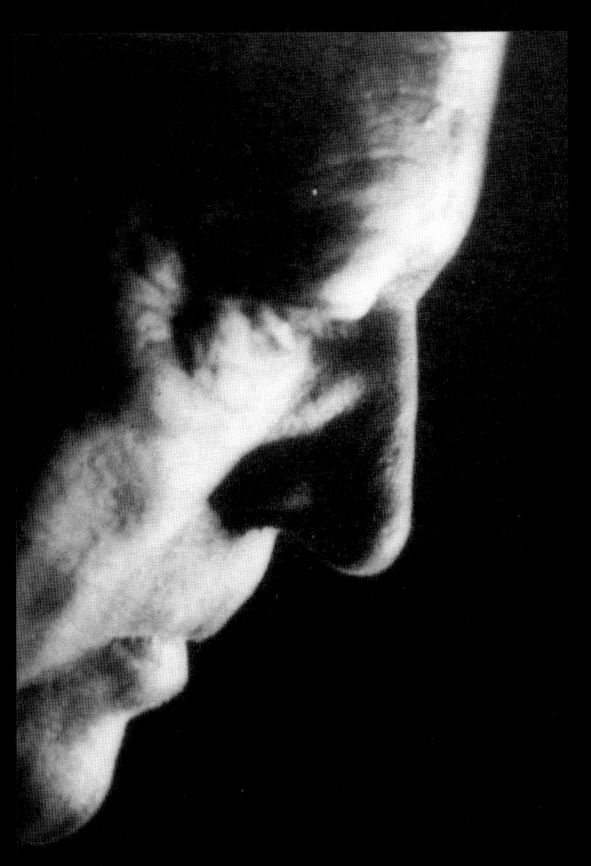

Without spectacles, on the other hand, the gaze goes all over the place.
Nothing shields or retains it as it flows freely forth and is absorbed and spread among the debris of the world.

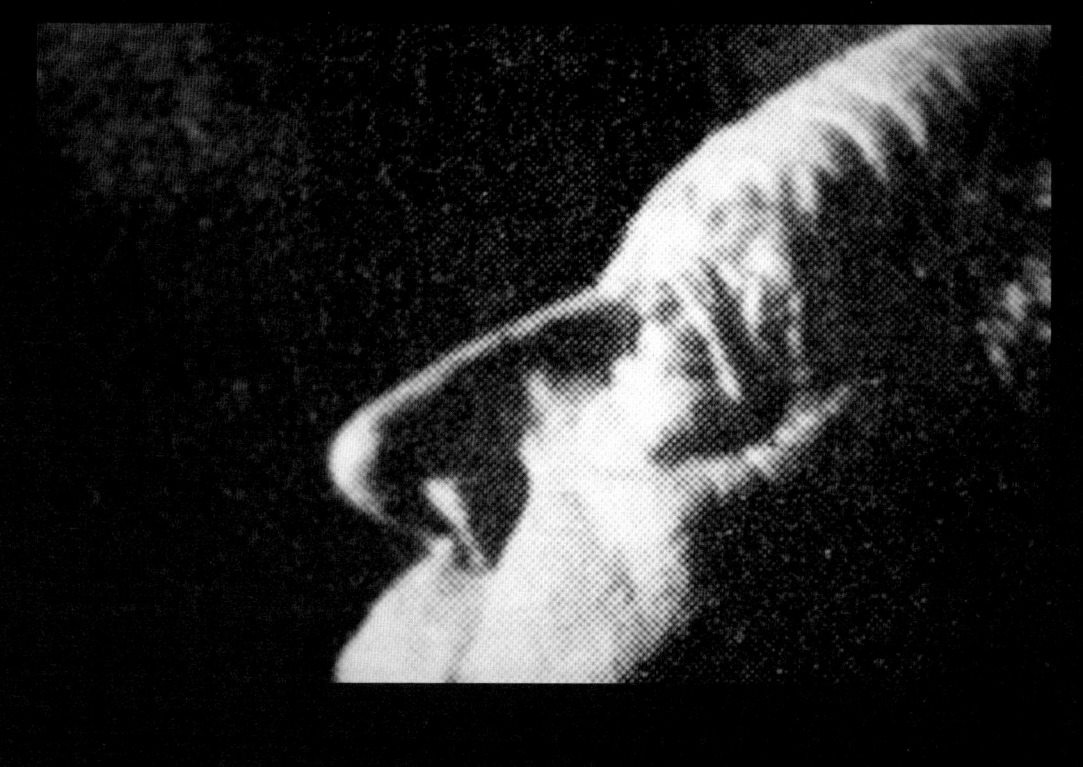

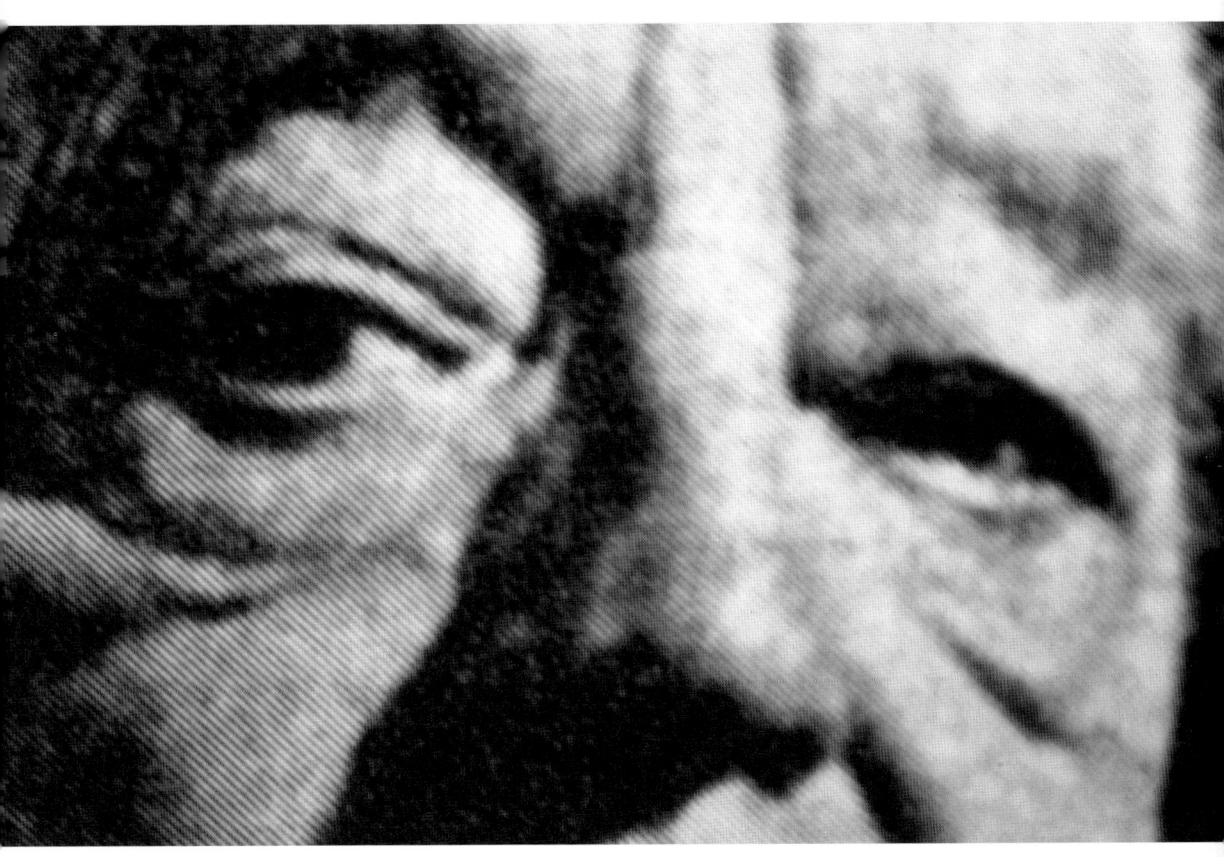

The gaze without spectacles retains nothing. From the eyes there flows something more unsteady and volatile than sails, springs, vapors, lodes.

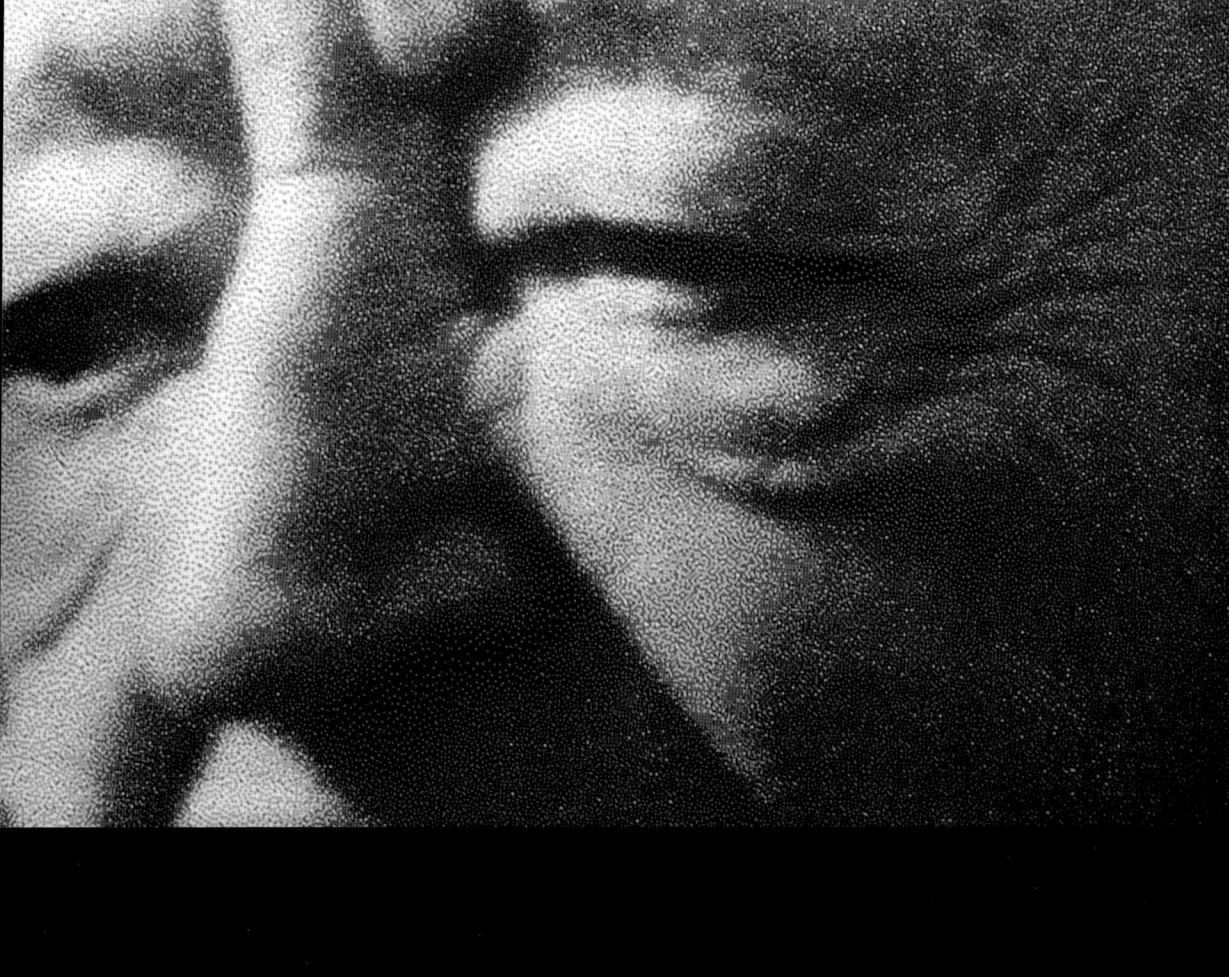

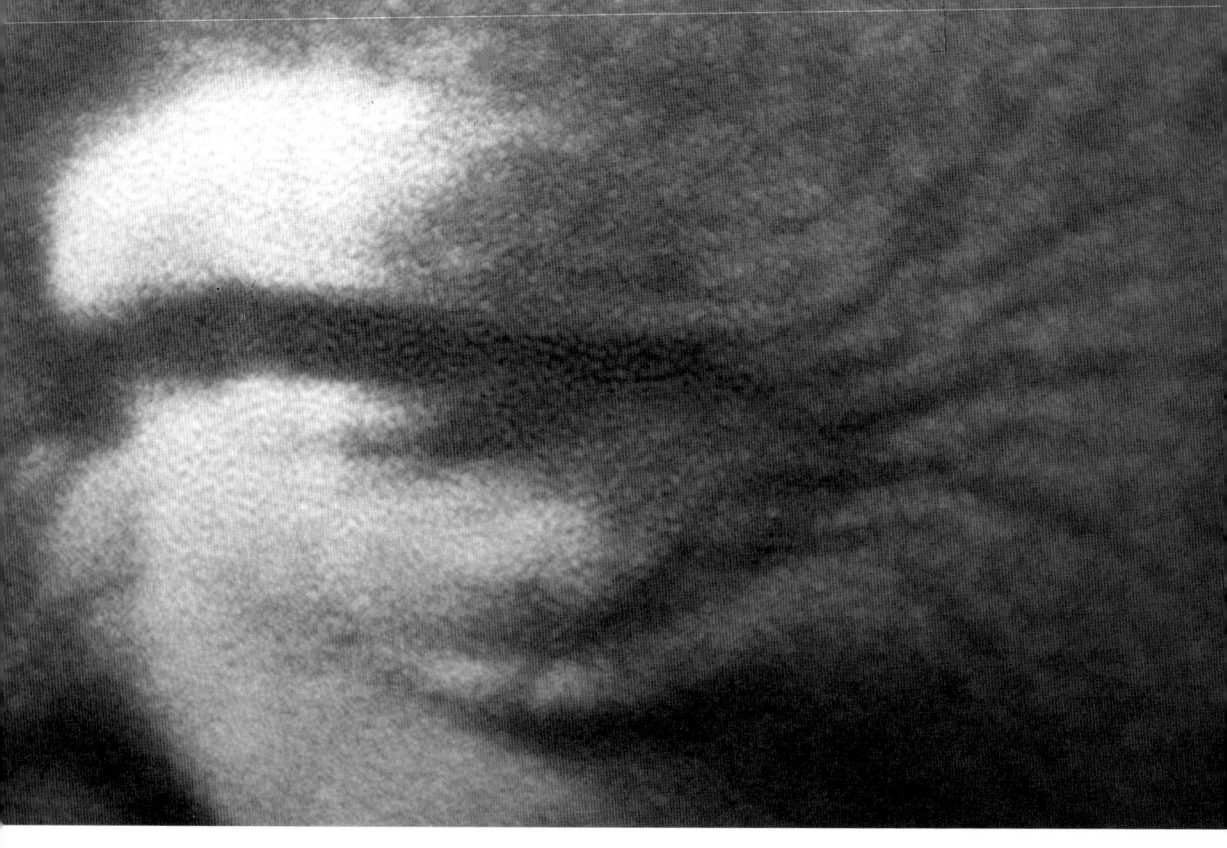

With advancing age and on account of his strabismus the sensation disappeared for Mies of the three-dimensional nature of objects, his eyes began to swivel, the pupil concealing itself beneath the eyelid; he was looking and experiencing through spots and diffuse and semi-transparent areas of opacity.

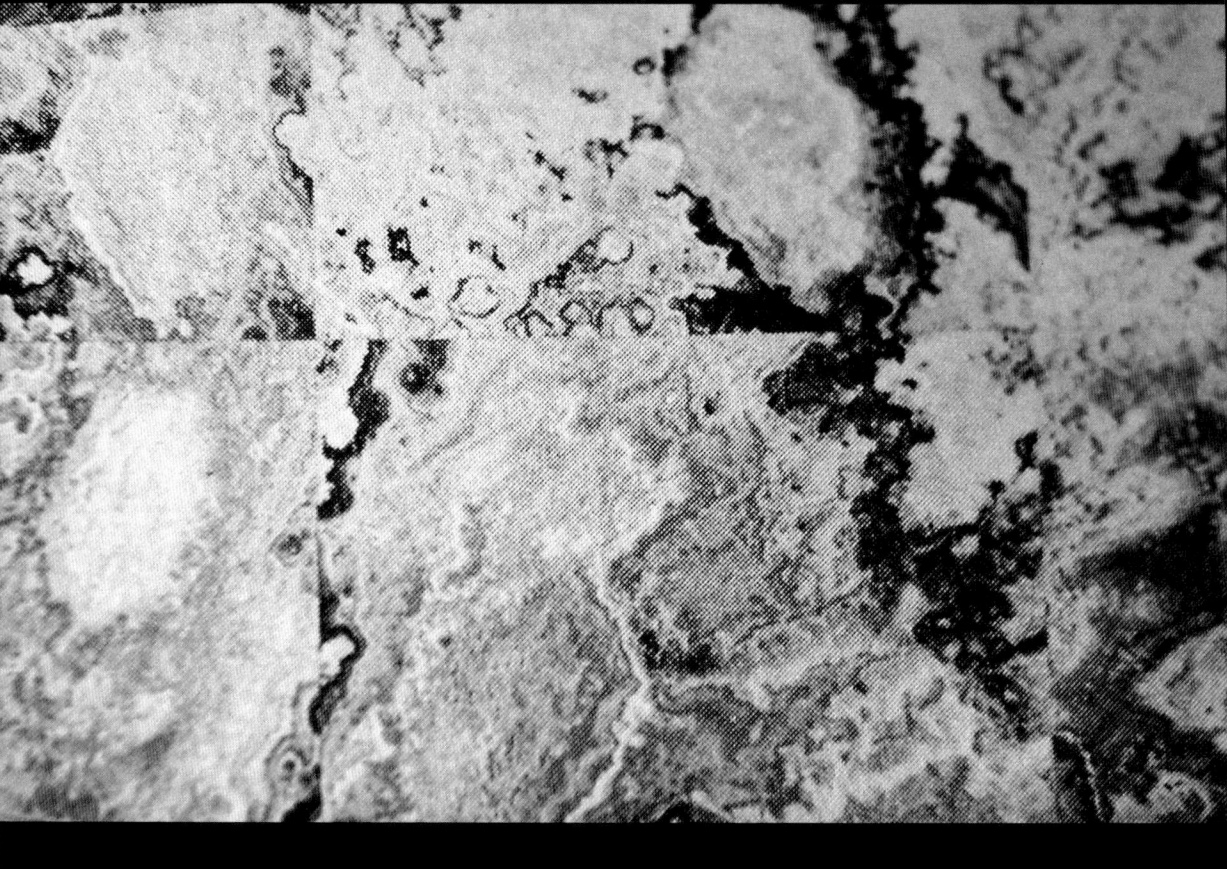

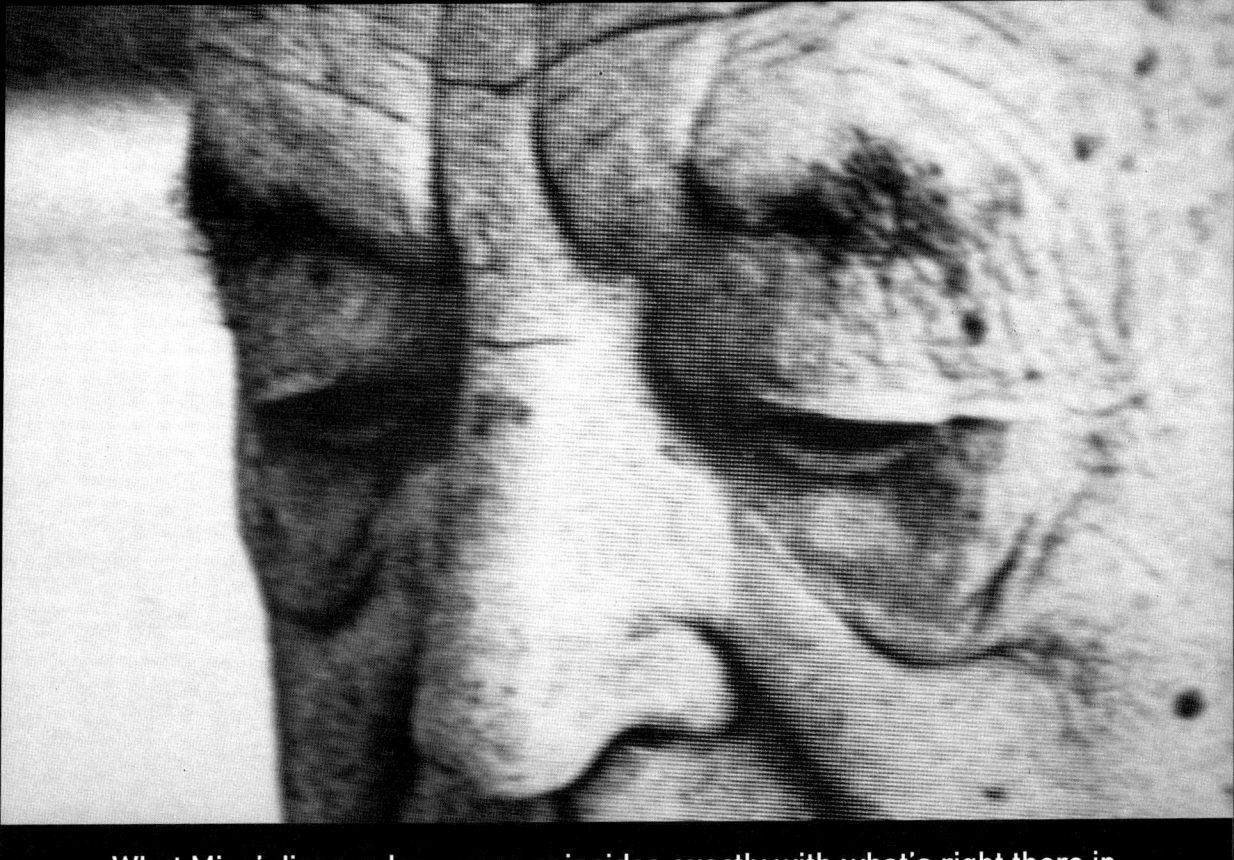

What Mies' diseased eyes see coincides exactly with what's right there in front of them, with what any Mies wall has, shows and is.

And when the wall is absent, the smoke from his Montecristo cigar makes up for it. World, eye and architecture are now one.

Perhaps Mies no longer needs to look.

What is Mies van der Rohe looking at?
Where is he?

1. The Hedrich-Blessing company was founded by Ken Hedrich and Hank Blessing and set up in Chicago in 1929. In 1930 Ed Hedrich joined as printer, manager and occasional photographer and in 1931 Bill Hedrich as professional photographer. From its beginnings and up to the present day the company has specialized in photographing architecture. Some of its best work is of the oeuvres of Frank Lloyd Wright and Saarinen, and much of Mies van der Rohe's. The Hedrich-Blessing studio subsequently expanded to include new photographers, among them the youngest member of the Hedrich family, Jack O. Hedrich, and Bill Engdahl, author of the photograph we present here. During an interchange of letters with Jack Hedrich, honorary chairman of Hedrich-Blessing, we were able to ascertain the following about the life and work of Bill Engdahl:

"Engdahl was a photographer with Hedrich-Blessing from the late 1950s to his retirement in 1985. He was not schooled in his trade, but began with Hedrich-Blessing as a photographer's apprentice after graduating from Senn High School in 1943. Later he became manager of the production department for several years. On his own time he began making photographs of nature and architecture, using equipment from the company. Beginning in middle 1950s Engdahl was given an occasional small job shooting architectural subjects when the other members of the staff had a crowded schedule. By 1959 Bill was shooting full time for many architectural clients. His was an unusual personality, and one that often did not fit into the normal concepts of what a Hedrich Blessing photographer should be and how he should act. Notwithstanding these idiosyncrasies, Bill Engdahl had a creative eye, as evidenced by the fact that any retrospective exhibit of the work of the firm from the 1960s through the 1980s will include several images of this talented artist..." Email from Hedrich Blessing. <hedrich@hedrich-blessing.com> Tuesday 1 June 1999, 08:36 a.m.

"Bill Engdahl passed away in April of 1997 at age 71. He was born and spent all of his life in Chicago. He attended Senn High School, graduating in June of 1943. He did not serve in the military as he was afflicted with epilepsy, which was kept under control for his lifetime with medication. He had no formal art or photography schooling." Email from Hedrich Blessing <hedrich@hedrich-blessing.com > Thursday 1 July 1999, 02:21 p.m.

"Bill Engdahl died in April of 1997." Email from Hedrich Blessing. <hedrich@hedrich-blessing.com> Tuesday 3 August 1999, 09:31 a.m.

2. In the Spanish edition of his book *Maestros de la arquitectura*, Peter Blake chose three splendid images of the three maestros Le Corbusier, Mies and Wright. Unfortunately, the photo of Mies on page 148 is the wrong way round. We know this, once again, through the position of the breast pocket of his jacket. (Peter Blake: *Maestros de la Arquitectura*, Editorial Victor Lerú, 3rd revised and updated edition, Buenos Aires 1973).

3. Various writers have remarked that Mies literally buried the Design Institute in the building's semi-basement as a result of his strong differences with László Moholy-Nagy, differences that went back to the time of the Bauhaus. Cf. Fritz Neumeyer, *The Artless Word, Mies van der Rohe, on the Building Art*, The MIT Press, Cambridge, Massachusetts London, England 1991, p. 134 and Franz Schulze, *Mies van der Rohe. A Critical Biography*, The University of Chicago Press, Chicago and London 1985, p. 342.

4. Once again, someone may be evaluating the possibility that the photograph with the students is the wrong way round. It cannot be, because we wouldn't see the hazy outline of certain buildings in the distance. If the photograph were the wrong way round we would inevitably see the Library & Administration building, which was constructed by a consortium in contradiction to Mies' plans, plus the Electrical Engineering & Physics building of which we will speak later.

5. And goes on to say: "If Ludwig's eye has been celebrated by generations of architecture historians, Ewald's was help in awe among the stonemasons of Aachen." Franz Schulze, op. cit., p. 16.

6. The confirmation that these two photographs were taken the same day as ours comes to us from Jack Hedrich himself. In the letter from Tuesday 1 June, quoted above, Jack Hedrich describes the context in which the photos were taken:
"A case in point is the photograph in which you have interest – of Mies van der Rohe stoically gazing into the distance while smoking one of his beloved cigars. Here is the scenario of how the photograph was made. Bill was making photographs of the interior of the newly completed Crown Hall at the Illinois Institute of Technology in Chicago for the Mies van der Rohe office. Being one of his most important projects both in design and personal involvement, Mies came to the photo session to supervise. At one time, when Engdahl was directing, from the camera, the lengthy process of setting up lighting, he noticed Mies sitting on a stool near the windows, seemingly lost in reverie. Without any commotion, Bill focused the camera on Mies and made two exposures on large, 8x10 inch film, before returning to the task at hand. Later in the same session, Bill suggested to Mies that a photograph be made of him at Crown Hall, and several other images were made. None, however, had the character and interest that appear in the photograph about which you inquire. In fact, an enlargement of that picture hangs in our conference room, with Mies looking across the room at another shot of Engdahls, an amazing photograph of the Dirksen Federal Center with extraordinary reflections in the glass facade. I hope this information is helpful to you, Mr. Daza. Good luck with your project."
Email from Hedrich Blessing <hedrich@hedrich-blessing.com> Tuesday 1 June 1999, 08:36 a.m.

7. Michael Mies and Amalia Rohe were the parents of a family of five children: Ewald Philipp (b. 13 October 1877); Carl Michael (b. 18 May 1879), who died at the age of 2; Anna Maria Elisabeth (b. 16 September 1881); Maria Johanna Sophie (b. 30 December 1883); and finally Maria Ludwig Michael Mies Rohe, born 27 March 1886 in Aachen, subsequently known as Ludwig Mies van der Rohe. It is worth pointing out that in his given name those of two of his siblings are to be found. The 'Maria' and 'Michael' will later disappear, and Mies will end up linking his paternal surnames with a *van der*: Mies van der Rohe. At a certain moment in his life he added a diaeresis to the *e* – Miës – to avoid the pejorative meanings of his forename in German: alarmist, defeatist, contempt, disdain, scorn, disparagement, inconsiderate-ness, etc. The diaeresis obviated the pronunciation *mis* for *mies*, now with two syllables. For all that, it appears that this contrivance didn't survive the 1930s. He would finally be known as Mies van der Rohe, or Mies as he seems to have been called, and went on being called, by everybody. We are now aware that, with or without a diaeresis, Mies' life and work have altered the German meaning of his given name for us.

8. Leucoma is the name for those opaque spots on the cornea which are generally the result of queriatitis ulcerosa. Both pannus and queriatitis parenquimatosa give rise to widespread, semi-transparent areas of opacity. Suppurating and malignant queriatitis each produce a pearly-white opaqueness consisting of sclerotic tissue. If an abscess on the cornea happens to result, ending in perforation, a thick white scar accompanied by piercing of the iris is the consequence. The visual disorders provoked by spots on the cornea depend on the thickness of the former, as well as on their size and location. If the spot occupies the whole of the pupil no image can be formed on the retina and vision is lost. Only when the spot is somewhat transparent can vision continue, although it will be misty and blurred. Astigmatism, strabismus and myopia often accompany corneal spots.

List and credits of the photographs:

It is necessary to clarify that many photographs have been cut out and close-ups have been performed on them with the sole purpose of emphasising some particular aspect of the work or the personality of Mies van der Rohe. It is also necessary to mention that all of the photographs presented here have been drawn out from documents, books and publications dealing on the life and work of Mies van der Rohe, without having visited Chicago and with no direct contact whatsoever with the building.
Every effort has been made to trace copyright holders. Any errors or omissions are inadvertent, and will be corrected in subsequent editions upon notification in writing to the publisher.

5: Original photo from the Chicago Historical Society. Clark Street at North Avenue Chicago, Illinois.
The picture has been published in the following magazines:
Architectural Forum, no. 8, August, 1956, p. 104.
Two years later, it was published in *Architecture d'Aujourd'hui*, no. 79, 1958, p. 1.
Seventeen years later, it was published on the cover of *Hogar y arquitectura*, no. 108-109, September – December issue of 1973.
And twenty-five years later in *A+U*, no. 124, 1981, p. 33.

7: The Crown Hall:
Mies Reconsidered: His Career, Legacy, and Disciples, The Art Institute of Chicago-Rizzoli International Publications 1986, p. 28.
Casabella, no. 214, 1957, p. 7.

8: Mies standing by the scale model of the Crown Hall:
Mies van der Rohe: architect as educator,

Illinois Institute of Technology 1986, Catalogue of the exhibition, p. 2.

9: Aerial view of the Project for the Illinois Institute of Technology:
Lorenzo Papi, *Ludwig Mies van der Rohe, Il Maestri del Novecento*, Firence 1975, p. 23.
"Plastico generale del campus dell'IIT a Chicago".
Photo Hedrich-Blessing.

10 above: Scale model:
Ludwing Hilbersaimer, *Mies van der Rohe*, Paul Theobald and Company, Chicago 1956, p. 166.
Model View.

10 bottom: Night view:
Peter Carter, *Mies van der Rohe at Work*, Pall Mall Press, London 1974, p. 80.
Crown Hall, Illinois Institute of Technology, Chicago: 1950-6. Night-time view.

12: The emery-polished glass edging:
Architectural Forum, no. 8, August, 1956, p. 104.

13 above: The entrance:
Carl W. Condit, *The Chicago School of Architecture*, Chicago and London 1964, ilus. 190, 1st ed. 1952.
Crown Hall, Illinois Institute of Technology, 1955-56. Ludwig Mies van der Rohe, Page Associates.
Photo Hube Henry, Hedrich-Blessing Studio; Illinois Institute of Technology.

13 bottom: The Crown Hall under construction:
Casabella, no. 214, 1957, p. 11.
Schulze-Danforth, *The Mies van der Rohe Archive*, Vol. 5, Book 12, p. 211.
IIT S.R. Crown Hall.
Mies van der Rohe: architect as educator,
Illinois Institute of Technology 1986, p. 117.

S.R. Crown Hall, Illinois Institute of Technology, Chicago.
Under Construction. c. 1955.
Photo Hedrich-Blessing.

15 above: Crown Hall, IIT Night view of the southern wing:
Schulze-Danforth, *The Mies van der Rohe Archive*, Vol. 5, Book 12, p. 208.
IIT S.R. Crown Hall.
Peter Carter, *Mies van der Rohe at Work*, Pall Mall Press, London 1974, pp. 88-89.
Crown Hall, IIT Exterior view from the south at night.
David Spaeth, *Mies van der Rohe*, Rizzoli, New York 1985, p. 153.
Crown Hall. Exterior.

15 bottom: Northern entrance:
Architectural Record, no. 237, August, 1956, p. 136.

16: The metal transom:
Architectural Forum, no. 8, August, 1956, p. 104.

17 left: The metal structure:
Peter Carter, *Mies van der Rohe at Work*, Pall Mall Press, London 1974, p. 12.
Crown Hall, IIT Chicago: 1950-56. Construction photograph.

17 right: The metal structure:
David Spaeth, *Mies van der Rohe*, Rizzoli, New York 1985, p. 150.
Crown Hall under construction.

18: The metal structure:
Werner Blaser, *Mies van der Rohe. Die Kunst der Struktur. L'art de la structure*, Artemis Verlag und Verlag für Architektur, Zurich and Stuttgart 1965, p. 92.
Horizontalschnitt. Maßstab $1/2$" = 1'– 0" (1:25)
Coupe horizontale. $1/2$ " = 1'– 0" (1:25).

19 left: Detail of the larger metal transom:
Schulze-Danforth, *The Mies van der Rohe
Archive*, Vol. 5, Book 12, p. 277.
Window detail. Section. Pencil on paper. 40 $^1/_2$"
x 42" (102.8 x 206.7 cm).
Dated: August 12, 1954. Archive: 5001.7
Neg: F.1078-10. "IIT S.R. Crown Hall".

19 right: Detail of the smaller metal transom:
Schulze-Danforth, *The Mies van der Rohe
Archive*, Vol. 5, Book 12, p. 276.
Window detail. Section. Pencil, coloured pencil
(red) on paper. 41 $^1/_4$" x 42" (104.8 x 106.7 cm).
Dated: August 12, 1954. Archive: 5001.4
Neg: F.1078-5. "IIT S.R. Crown Hall".

20: The tree branches:
Architectural Forum, no. 8, August, 1956,
p. 104.

21: Crown Hall ground floor:
David Spaeth, *Mies van der Rohe*, Rizzoli,
New York 1985, p. 148.
Crown Hall, IIT, 1950-56. Upper level plan.

22: Aerial view of the building:
Global Architecture, no. 14, p. 39.

24: The joints of the paving tiles:
Architectural Forum, no. 8, August 1956, p. 104.

26: The square-shaped tiles:
Architecture d'Aujourd'hui, no. 79, 1958, p. 48.

27: The rectangular tiles:
Architectural Record, no. 237, August, 1956,
p. 133.

28: Construction detail of the tiles:
Schulze-Danforth, *The Mies van der Rohe
Archive*, Vol. 5, Book 12, p. 266.
Plan of wood walls at offices and library.
Pencil on paper. 21" x 40" (53.3 x 101.6 cm).
Dated: October 4, 1954. Archive: 5001.20
Neg: F.843-15.

30: The trimming around the ceiling:
Architectural Forum, no. 8, August 1956, p. 104.

31: The structure:
Casabella, no. 214, 1957, p. 11.
View of the structure during assembly.
After the four large plate girders are
assembled, the beams and sheet steel roof
are then suspended from the main structure.

32: The Structure:
Casabella, no. 214, 1957, p. 11.

32/33: The structure:
Architectural Forum, no. 8, August 1956,
p. 109.

33: The structure:
*Mies Reconsidered: His Career, Legacy, and
Disciples*, The Art Institute of Chicago-Rizzoli
International Publications, New York 1986,
p. 28.
Crown Hall, IIT, Chicago 1950-56, under
construction.

34: Detail of suspended ceiling:
Ludwing Hilbersaimer, *Mies van der Rohe*,
Paul Theobald and Company, Chicago 1956,
p. 171-172.
Vertical Sections through building and
horizontal section through building.

35, 36, 37, 38: The same photograph taken by
Bill Engdahl of Hedrich-Blessing reveals a
small detail.
A+U, no. 124, 1981, p. 33.

40. Our picture, inverted:
A+U, no. 124, 1981, p. 33.

41 left: Sequence of inverted photographs
of Mies :
Werner Blaser, *Il design di Mies van der Rohe,
Mobili e interni*, Electa Editrice, Milano 1980,
p. 11.

"Nella sua abitazione di East Pearson Street a
Chicago, alle sue spalle il quadro di Paul
Klee", 1964.

41 right: Mies correctly published:
Franz Schulze, *A Critical Biography*,
The University of Chicago Press, Chicago and
London 1985, p. 314.
Mies in his apartment with painting by Paul
Klee and sculpture by Pablo Picasso.
Fritz Neumeyer, *Mies van der Rohe,
Das kunstlose Wort, Gedanken zur Baukunst*,
Sedler Verlag, Berlin 1986, p. 402.
Mies in his apartment in Chicago.

42: Close-up on the leaf:
Franz Schulze, *A Critical Biography*,
The University of Chicago Press, Chicago
and London 1985, p. 314.
Mies in his apartment with painting by Paul
Klee and sculpture by Pablo Picasso.

43: Paul Klee's painting behind Mies:
Werner Blaser, *Il design di Mies van der Rohe,
Mobili e interni*, Electa Editrice, Milano 1980,
p. 11.
Nella sua abitazione di East Pearson Street a
Chicago, alle sue spalle il quadro di Paul Klee,
1964.

44 left: Our picture, inverted:
A+U, no. 124, 1981, p. 33.

44 right: Our picture, inverted:
Architectural Forum, no. 8, August 1956, p. 104.

45: Coming closer to Mies:
Architectural Forum, no. 8, August 1956, p. 104.

46: Mies, always impeccable:
*Mies van der Rohe Architecture and Design in
Stuttgart, Barcelona*, Brno, Vitra Design
Museum-Skira editore 1998, p. 216.
Mies in his apartment on East Pearson Street,
Chicago 1964.

47: Coming closer to the handkerchief :
Architectural Forum, no. 8, August, 1956,
p. 104.

48 left: Coming closer to Mies, inverted:
Architectural Forum, no. 8, August, 1956,
p. 104.

48 right: Coming closer to Mies:
Architectural Forum, no. 8, August, 1956,
p. 104.

50: The Shadows:
Architectural Forum, no. 8, August, 1956,
p. 104.

51: The closed blind:
Architectural Forum, no. 8, August, 1956,
p. 104.

52: Crown Hall interior:
Architecture d'Aujourd'hui, no. 79, 1958, p. 45.

53: Crown Hall interior:
Architectural Forum, no. 8, August, 1956,
p. 105.

54: Crown Hall interior:
Peter Carter, *Mies van der Rohe at Work*,
Pall Mall Press, London 1974, p. 90.
Crown Hall. IIT Interior View.

55: Crown Hall interior:
Mies van der Rohe: architect as educator,
Illinois Institute of Technology 1986, p. 64.
Alfred Caldwell with class in S. R. Crown Hall.
C. 1956.

56: Crown Hall interior:
Global, no. 14, p. 37.

57: Crown Hall Interior:
David Spaeth, *Mies van der Rohe*, Rizzoli,
New York 1985, p. 151.
Crown Hall. Interior.

58: Crown Hall interior:
Franz Schulze, *A Critical Biography*,
The University of Chicago Press, Chicago
and London 1985, p. 323.
Mies memorial service at IIT, 1968.
In foreground, left to right, Dirk Lohan,
James Johnson Sweeney, Lora Marx,
Marianne Lohan, Laura Sweeney, Phyllis
Lambert, Philip Johnson.

59: Crown Hall interior – Mies – John Rettaliata:
Mies van der Rohe: architect as educator,
Illinois Institute of Technology 1986, Catalogue
of the exhibition, p. 119.
S.R. Crown Hall Dedication, Illinois Institute of
Technology. 30 April 1956. John Rettaliata,
President of IIT with Mies.

60 left: The lower ground floor:
Architectural Record, no. 237, August, 1956,
p. 137.
Typical design workshop.
Chicago Architectural Photographing
Company.

60 center: The lower ground floor:
Architectural Record, no. 237, August, 1956,
p. 139.
A corridor to Design.
Chicago Architectural Photographing
Company.

60 right: Staircase leading to the lower
ground floor:
Casabella, no. 214, 1957, p. 10.
Une vue du hall du sous-sol avec l'escalier
métallique qui conduit à l'étage principal.

62: Outdoor staircase leading to lower
ground floor:
Architectural Record, no. 237, August, 1956,
p. 138.
For deliveries.
Chicago Architectural Photographing
Company.

63: Outside corner:
Architecture d'Aujourd'hui, no. 79, 1958, p. 79.

64: Staircase on southern section:
Architectural Forum, no. 8, August, 1956, p. 107.
Entrance has classical character, without
historical debris. Porch is an eminent
gathering place, observation platform and
reviewing stand for students between classes.
Low penthouse is for mechanical equipment.
Photo Richard Pytlik.

65: Staircase on northern section:
Casabella, no. 214, 1957, p. 11.
Veduta della Crown Hall da nord.

66: Lower ground floor ground plan:
Architectural Forum, no. 8, August, 1956,
p. 110.
Basement Plan.

68: The students:
Schulze-Danforth, *The Mies van der Rohe
Archive*, Vol. 5, Book 12, p. 209.
IIT S.R. Crown Hall.

71 above: Farther away from the students:
Schulze-Danforth, *The Mies van der Rohe
Archive*, Vol. 5, Book 12, p. 209.
IIT S.R. Crown Hall.

71 bottom: Even farther away from the
students:
Schulze-Danforth, *The Mies van der Rohe
Archive*, Vol. 5, Book 12, p. 209.
IIT S.R. Crown Hall.

72 left: Mies' Birthday:
Mies van der Rohe: architect as educator,
Illinois Institute of Technology 1986, p. 146.
Eight images of Mies's 75th Birthday. Party at
Charles's Genther's Apartment, 860 Lake
Shore Drive. Chicago. 1961. Polaroid.
Photographs lent by George Danforth.

72 right: Crown Hall ground plan:
David Spaeth, *Mies van der Rohe*, Rizzoli,
New York 1985, p. 148.
Crown Hall, IIT, 1950-56. Upper level plan.
Fritz Neumeyer, *Mies van der Rohe. The word
with no artifice*, Madrid 1995, p. 332.
Crown Hall, IIT, Chicago 1950-1956.

73: Mies and the Crown Hall scale model:
Carter Wiseman, *Shaping a Nation, Twentieth
– Century American Architecture and its
Makers*, Hong Kong 1988, p. 173.

74: Even farther away from the students:
Schulze-Danforth, *The Mies van der Rohe
Archive*, Vol. 5, Book 12, p. 209.
IIT S.R. Crown Hall.

75: The students:
Schulze-Danforth, *The Mies van der Rohe
Archive*, Vol. 5, Book 12, p. 209.
IIT S.R. Crown Hall.

79: A faint sketch drawn by Mies:
Mies van der Rohe: architect as educator,
Illinois Institute of Technology 1986, p. 117.
Ludwig Mies van der Rohe, Joseph Fijikawa.
Eight sketch for S.R. Crown Hall. Illinois
Institute of Technology. Early 1950's. Pencil on
note paper. 6" x 8 1/4" (15.1 x 21.1 cm).

80: Mies van der Rohe:
Architectural Forum, no. 8, August, 1956, p.104.

84: Our photograph:
Architectural Forum, no. 8, August, 1956, p.104.

86: Our photograph:
Architectural Forum, no. 8, August, 1956,
p.104.

87: Mies holding the cigar in his right hand:
*Mies Reconsidered: His Career, Legacy, and
Disciples*, The Art Institute of Chicago-Rizzoli
International Publications 1986, p. 11.

Mies van der Rohe in an apartment at 860
Lake Shore Drive, c. 1952.
Fritz Neumeyer, *Mies van der Rohe.
Das kunstlose Wort, Gedanken zur Baukunst*,
Sedler Verlag, Berlin 1986, p. 382.
Mies um 1950.

88: Mies holding the cigar in his right hand:
Werner Blaser, *Il design di Mies van der Rohe,
Mobili e interni*, Electa Editrice, Milano 1980,
p. 8.
Mies nello studio di East Ohio Street a Chicago
1964.

89: Mies holding the cigar in his right hand:
Architectural Design A.D. no. 3/4, March -
April, 1995, p. 30.
Ludwig Mies van der Rohe and Philip Johnson
in front of the Seagram Building, New York
1959.

90: Mies holding the cigar in his right hand:
Daniela Hammer-Tugendhat/Wolf Tegethoff,
*Ludwig Mies van der Rohe. The Tugendhat
House*, Springer-Verlag, Wien-New York,
2000, p. 28.
Tugendhat House, Mies van der Rohe in the
living room.

91: Mies holding the cigar in his right hand:
Franz Schulze, *A Critical Biography*, The
University of Chicago Press, Chicago and
London 1985, p. 315.
Four generations: Mies with Marianne, Dirk
Lohan, and Dirk's children, Caroline and Lars,
mid-1960s.

92: Mies holding the cigar in his right hand:
Architecture d'Aujourd'hui, no. 79, 1958,
p. XLXIX.
Photo Hedrich-Blessing
«Less is more» «moins est plus».
Hogar y arquitectura, no. 108-109, September
- December, 1973, p. 114.
Another picture of Mies by Hedrich-Blessing,

one of the most outstanding photographers of
Life magazine.

93: Mies holding the cigar in his right hand:
Architectural Monographs, no. 11, 1986, pp. 6-7.
Mies van der Rohe.

94: Mies holding the cigar in his right hand:
Mies van der Rohe: architect as educator,
Illinois Institute of Technology 1986, Catalogue
of the exhibition, p. 146.
Three images of Hilbersaimer's day. Party 21
December 1961. Colour photographs. 2 3/8" x
3 3/8" (6,6 x 8,7cm). Lent by George Danforth.

95: Mies holding the cigar in his right hand:
Franz Schulze, *A Critical Biography*,
The University of Chicago Press, Chicago and
London 1985, p. 234.
Mies and Lora Marx at a New Year's Eve party
at the home of Charles and Margrette
Dornbusch, Chicago 1940.

96: Close up to the right hand:
Franz Schulze, *A Critical Biography*,
The University of Chicago Press, Chicago and
London 1985, p. 234.
Mies and Lora Marx at a New Year's Eve party
at the home of Charles and Margrette
Dornbusch, Chicago 1940.

97, 98: Mies standing by his brother Ewald, the
hands and the match:
Franz Schulze, *A Critical Biography*,
The University of Chicago Press, Chicago and
London 1985, p. 294.
Ewald Mies and Mies at the Schlosshotel
Guelpen, The Netherlands 1961.

99: Mies sketching with his right hand:
Wolf Tegethoff, *Mies van der Rohe. Die Villen
und Landhausprojekte*, Bonn 1981, p. 60.
Mies van der Rohe während der Arbeit am
Haus Esters.
Franz Schulze, *A Critical Biography*,

The University of Chicago Press, Chicago and London 1985, p. 147.
Mies working on a drawing of the Esters House.

100: Mies holding the cigar in his left hand:
Architectural Forum, no. 8, August, 1956, p.104.

101 left: Mies in his apartment on East Pearson Street, Chicago:
Werner Blaser, *Mies van der Rohe. The Art of Structure. Die Kunst der Struktur*, Birkhäuser-Verlag für Architektur, Basel, Boston, Berlin 1993, p. 7.
The German and English texts to this new and expanded edition were originally published in 1965.

101 right: Mies in his apartment on East Pearson Street, Chicago:
Werner Blaser, *Mies van der Rohe. Die Kunst der Struktur, L'art de la structure*, Artemis Verlag und Verlag für Architektur, Zurich and Stuttgart 1965, p. 7.

103 left: Mies in his apartment on East Pearson Street, Chicago:
Werner Blaser, *Mies van der Rohe. The Art of Structure. Die Kunst der Struktur*, Birkhäuser-Verlag für Architektur, Basel, Boston, Berlin 1993, p. 7.

103 right: Mies in his apartment on East Pearson Street, Chicago:
Werner Blaser, *Mies van der Rohe. Die Kunst der Struktur, L'art de la structure*, Artemis Verlag und Verlag für Architektur, Zurich and Stuttgart 1965, p. 7.

104: Mies drawing with his right hand:
Wolf Tegethoff, *Mies van der Rohe. Die Villen und Landhausprojekte*, Bonn 1981, p. 62.
Mies van der Rohe während der Arbeit am Haus Esters.

105: Mies lighting a cigar:
Mies Reconsidered: His Career, Legacy, and Disciples, The Art Institute of Chicago-Rizzoli International Publications 1986, p. 32.
Mies van der Rohe at the opening of Cullinan Hall, Museum of Fine Arts, October 1958.

106: Mies holding the cigar in his left hand:
Franz Schulze, *A Critical Biography*, The University of Chicago Press, Chicago and London 1985, p. 237.
Mies, Philip Johnson, and Phyllis Lambert, mid-1950s.

107 left: Mies holding the cigar in his left hand:
Franz Schulze, *A Critical Biography*, The University of Chicago Press, Chicago and London 1985, p. 269.
Mies studying model of Convention Hall.

107 right: Mies holding the cigar in his left hand:
Mies van der Rohe: architect as educator, Illinois Institute of Technology 1986, Catalogue of the exhibition, p. 115.
Mies at Open House Exhibit, Alumni. Memorial Hall, Illinois Institute of Technology, 1949.

108: Mies holding the cigar in his left hand:
Franz Schulze, *A Critical Biography*, The University of Chicago Press, Chicago and London 1985, p. 290.
Waltraut Mies van der Rohe and Ludwig Mies, Chicago 1955.

109: Mies holding the cigar in his left hand:
Franz Schulze, *A Critical Biography*, The University of Chicago Press, Chicago and London 1985, p. 288.
Mies and Harry Weese at the Graham Foundation, ca. 1962.

110 left: Mies holds the cigar with his other hand:
Werner Blaser, *Mies van der Rohe.*
Less is more, Waser Verlag Zurich 1986, New York, p. 34.
Mies in seinem Büro an der East Ohio Street in Chicago 1964.
Mies in his office in East Ohio Street in Chicago 1964.

110 right: Mies holds the cigar with his other hand:
Werner Blaser, *Mies van der Rohe. Less is more*, Waser Verlag Zurich 1986, New York, p. 34.
Mies in seinem Büro an der East Ohio Street in Chicago 1964.
Mies in his office in East Ohio Street in Chicago 1964.

111: Mies standing by his brother Ewald:
Franz Schulze, *A Critical Biography*, The University of Chicago Press, Chicago and London 1985, p. 290.
Ewald Mies and Ludwig Mies at Miesville, Wisconsin, 1957.

113 left: Another picture which was taken on the same day as ours:
Peter Carter, *Mies van der Rohe at Work*, Pall Mall Press, London 1974, p. 173.
Mies van der Rohe in Crown Hall, (398 and Jacket) Bill Engdahl, Hedrich-Blessing 18506 K4.
David Spaeth, *Mies van der Rohe*, Rizzoli, New York 1985, p. 18.
Mies in Crown Hall, Illinois Institute of Technology, Chicago, Illinois, ca. 1958.
Sources of Illustration: Bill Engdahl, Hedrich-Blessing.
Domus, no. 674, July - August, 1986, p. 19.
Mies van der Rohe, fotografato a Chicago da Hedrich-Blessing.

113 right: Another picture that was taken on the same day as ours:
This picture has also been taken by Bill Engdahl, please refer to note 6.

185

115: Aerial view of the Institute
GA Global Architecture, no. 14, 1972, p. 40.

116: Illinois Institute of Technology:
Mies van der Rohe: architect as educator,
Illinois Institute of Technology 1986, Catalogue
of the exhibition. p. 61.
Illinois Institute of Technology campus model
with James C. Peebles, Mies van der Rohe,
Henry T. Heald.

117: Illinois Institute of Technology:
Architecture d'Aujourd'hui, no. 79, 1958, p. 28.
Plan d'ensemble: 1. Banc d'essai. 2. Chaufferie.
3. Transformateur. 4. Recherche métallurgi-
que. 5. Ingénieurs civils. 6. Physique et
Electricité. 7. Entretien. 8. Administration.
9. Equipement mécanique. 10. Recherche
mécanique. 13. Bibliothèque et administration.
14. Union des Etudiants. 15. and 16.
Laboratoirs. 17 Laboratoirs d'Ingénieurs.
18. Administration des Recherches.
19. Recherches physiques et électriques.
20. Laboratoires 21. Administration d'études
du gaz. 22. Faculté d'architecture.
23. Ingénieurs en mécanique. 24 Lewis Hall.
25. Faculté de Chimie. 26. Ingénieurs chimistes
et métallurgistes. 27. Alumini Memorial Hall.
28. and 29. Gymnases 30. Station-service.
31. Habitations. 32. Centre Comercial.
33 to 41. Groupes d'habitations individuelles
autour d'une maison commune.
42. Dortoirs jeunes filles. 43. Hall Harr.
44. 45. and 46. Dortoirs. 47. Fowler Hall.
48. Chapelle. 49. Carman Hall. 50. Gunsaulas
Hall. 51. Cunningham Hall. 52. Bailey Hall.
53. 54. 55. Immeubles collectifs.
It should be mentioned that some of the
purposes of the buildings have changed in
accordance with the different proposals for
the campus.

118 above, bottom: The campus field in 1944
and its transformation carried out in 1963:

Harold M. Mayer - Ricahrad C. Wade, *Chicago:
Growth of a Metropolis*, The University of
Chicago Press, Chicago and London 1969, p. 384.
View across the Illinois Institute of Technology
Campus, Corner of Thirty-First and Wabash,
1944 and 1963. Old houses surrounded the IIT
campus in 1944 when the first photograph
was taken, and some of the city's worst slums
were in immediate proximity to the campus.

119: Aerial views of the campus with the new
S.O.M. works:
*Mies Reconsidered: His Career, Legacy, and
Disciples*, The Art Institute of Chicago-Rizzoli
International Publications 1986, p. 78.
Aerial view of the campus at IIT, looking north,
1986.

120: Aerial view of the campus, Electric and
Physical Engineering Building:
*Mies Reconsidered: His Career, Legacy, and
Disciples*, The Art Institute of Chicago-Rizzoli
International Publications 1986, p. 78.
Aerial view of the campus at IIT, facing north,
1986.

121: The Engineering and Physics building
behind the Crown Hall:
*Mies van der Rohe. Masters of Modern
Architecture*, Introduction and notes by Martin
Pawley with photographs by Yukio Futagawa,
Thames and Hudson, London 1970, fig. 2.
Main entrance to Crown Hall, showing
travertine marble steps and platform terrace
as well the inner pair of steel upstand beams.

122: Mies:
Architectural Forum, no. 8, August, 1956, p. 104.

124: Mies' Glance:
Architectural Forum, no. 8, August, 1956, p. 104.

128: Aerial view of the northern side of the
building:

GA Global Architecture, no. 14, 1972, p. 38.

129, 130, 131: Original ground plans:
Schulze-Danforth, *The Mies van der Rohe
Archive*, Volume 4, Book 11, p. 354.
Site plan. Pencil on paper. 26" x 46"
(66 x 121.9 cm). Dated: September 4, 1957.
Archive: 5505.59. Neg: F-897-4.

133: Speculative designs of the Mechanical
Engineering building:
Schulze-Danforth, *The Mies van der Rohe
Archive*, Vol. 1, Book 8, p. 150.
IIT Speculative Designs, 1939. Mechanical
engineering building. Exterior perspective.
Sketch. Pencil, charcoal on tracing, 16" x 30"
(41.9 x 76.2cm). Archive: 3903.3. Neg: G-1852.

134: Speculative designs of the Mechanical
Engineering building:
Schulze-Danforth, *The Mies van der Rohe
Archive*, Vol. 1, Book 8, p. 150.
IIT Speculative Designs, 1939. Mechanical
engineering building. Exterior perspective.
Sketch. Pencil on paper. 21" x 40" (53.3 x
102.8cm). Archive: 3903.5. Neg: G-1907.

135: Speculative designs of the Mechanical
Engineering building:
Schulze-Danforth, *The Mies van der Rohe
Archive*, Vol. 1, Book 8, p. 150.
IIT Speculative Designs, 1939. Mechanical
engineering building. Exterior perspective.
Sketch. Pencil, charcoal on tracing, 15" x 34"
(38.1 x 86.3 cm). Archive: 3903.4. Neg: G-1904.

136: Speculative designs of the Mechanical
Engineering building:
Schulze-Danforth, *The Mies van der Rohe
Archive*, Vol. 1, Book 8, p. 149.
IIT Speculative Designs, 1939. Mechanical
engineering building. Exterior perspective.
Sketch. Pencil, charcoal on tracing, 16" x 30"
(41.9 x 76.2cm). Archive: 3903.2. Neg: G-1851.

137: Close-up on Mies:
Architectural Forum, no. 8, August, 1956, p.104.

138 left: Close-up on Mies:
Elain S. Hochman, *Architects of Fortune*,
From International Publishing Corporation
New York, p. 44. Mies, about 1912.

138 right: Close-up on Mies:
Fritz Neumeyer, *Mies van der Rohe*,
Das kunstlose Wort, Gedanken zur Baukunst,
Sedler Verlag, Berlin 1986, p. 296.
Mies um 1923.

140: Close-up on Mies:
Mies van der Rohe: architect as educator,
Illinois Institute of Technology 1986, Catalogue
for the exhibition, p. 115.
Mies at Open House Exhibit, Alumni. Memorial
Hall, Illinois Institute of Technology, 1949.

141: Close-up on Mies:
Architectural Monographs, no. 11, 1986, p. 2.
Mies van der Rohe, ca. 1930.

142: Close-up on Mies:
Architectural Forum, no. 5, November, 1952, p.93.

143: Close-up on Mies:
Mies van der Rohe: architect as educator,
Illinois Institute of Technology 1986, Catalogue
of the exhibition, p. 119.
S.R. Crown Hall dedication, Illinois Institute of
Technology 30 April 1956.
Photographs Arthur Siegel.

144: Close-up on Mies:
Werner Blaser, *Il design di Mies van der Rohe*,
Mobili e interni, Electa Editrice, Milano 1980, p. 6.

145: Close-up on:
Ludwing Hilbersaimer, *Mies van der Rohe*,
Italian edition by Antonio Monesteroli,
Titolo originale: Mies van der Rohe, 1956,

Paul Theobald and Company, traduzione
Antonio Monestiroli, p. 19.
Mies van der Rohe.

146: Mies' parents:
Franz Schulze, *A Critical Biography*,
The University of Chicago Press, Chicago and
London 1985, p. 11.
Mies's parents, Michael Mies and Amalie, née
Rohe, in 1921.

147: Close-up on Mies' eyes:
Elain S. Hochman, *Architecs of Fortune*,
Fromm International Publishing Corporation
New York, p. 44.
Mies, ca. 1912.

149 left: Close-up on Mies:
Ludwig Mies van der Rohe, *Escritos, diálogos
y discursos*, (Writings, dialogues and
speeches) Architecture Collection 1, Murcia
1981, p. 4.
Portrait of L. Mies van der Rohe.

149 right: Close-up on Mies:
Mies van der Rohe, Critical Essays. Edited by
Franz Schulze, The Museum of Art, New York
1989, p. 11.
Ludwig Mies van der Rohe, 1947.

150, 151: Mies surprised by Scherschel:
Architectural Forum, no. 4, April, 1960, p. 132.
Frank Scherschel-Life. A medal for L. Mies
van der Rohe.
Hogar y arquitectura, no. 108-109, September
- December, 1973, p. 112.
Mies van der Rohe photographed by Frank
Scherschel in his Chicago study, 1957.

152: Mies:
Mies van der Rohe, Critical Essays. Edited by
Franz Schulze, The Museum of Art, New York
1989, p. 11.
Ludwig Mies van der Rohe, 1947.

153: Close-up on Mies:
*Mies van der Rohe, Neue Nationalgalerie in
Berlin*, Vice Versa Verlag, 1995, p. 90.

154: Close-up on Mies' eyes:
Architecture d'Aujourd'hui, no. 79, 1958,
p. XLXIX. Photo Hedrich-Blessing.
«Less is more» «moins est plus».

155: Close-up on Mies' eyes:
Architectural Design A.D, no. 3-4 , March-
April, 1995, p. 30.

156: Close-up on Mies' eyes:
Philip Johnson, *Mies van der Rohe*, The
Museum of Modern Art, New York 1947, p. 8.
Mies van der Rohe.

157: Close-up on Mies' eyes:
*Mies Reconsidered: His Career, Legacy, and
Disciples*, The Art Institute of Chicago-Rizzoli
International Publications 1986.
Cover illustration: Robert Damora,
Autographed portrait photograph of Ludwig
Mies van der Rohe, c.1947.

158: Close-up on Mies' eyes:
Hogar y arquitectura, no. 108-109, September
- December, 1973, p. 113.
Mies van der Rohe photographed by
H. Blessing in 1957.

159: Close-up on Mies' eyes:
Architectural Forum, no. 4, April, 1960, p. 132.
Frank Scherschel-Life. A medal for L. Mies
van der Rohe.

160: Close-up on Mies' eyes:
Ludwing Hilbersaimer, *Mies van der Rohe*,
edizione italiana a cura di Antonio
Monesteroli, Titolo originale: Mies van der
Rohe, 1956, Paul Theobald and Company,
traduzione Antonio Monestiroli, p. 19.
Mies van der Rohe.

161: His eyes gradually disappeared:
Alison and Peter Smithson, *Changing the Art of Inhabitation*, Artemis, London Zurich
Munich 1994, p. 7.
Mies'pieces.

162: His eyes gradually disappeared:
Alison and Peter Smithson, *Changing the Art of Inhabitation*, Artemis, London Zurich
Munich 1994, p. 7.
Mies'pieces.

163: The reflection:
Franz Schulze, *A Critical Biography*,
The University of Chicago Press, Chicago and
London 1985, p. 314.
Mies in his apartment with painting by Paul
Klee and sculpture by Pablo Picasso.
Fritz Neumeyer, *Mies van der Rohe,
Das kunstlose Wort, Gedanken zur Baukunst*,
Sedler Verlag, Berlin 1986, p. 402.
Mies in seinem Apartment in Chicago.

164: A wall by Mies, in any building by Mies,
in any book on Mies.

165: His eyes gradually disappeared:
Franz Schulze, *A Critical Biography*,
The University of Chicago Press, Chicago and
London 1985, p. 317.
Mies reading *Bauen seit 1900 in Berlin*, by
Rave and Knöfel, 1967.
Photo Dirk Lohan.

166: The smoke from his cigar:
*Three centuries of Notable American
Architects*. Edited by Joseph J. Thorndike, JR.
Orbis Publishing, London 1982, p. 266.
Photo Frank Scherschel, *Life* magazine.

167–175: Close-up on Mies:
Architectural Forum, no. 8, August, 1956,
p. 104.

Author:
Ricardo Daza, Professor Universidad Nacional de Colombia
dazaricardo@hotmail.com

Graphic Design:
Ramon Prat, Anja Tränkel

Collaboration:
Anna Tetas

Translation from Spanish into English:
Paul Hammond

Production:
Actar Pro

Printing:
Ingoprint S. A.

Distribution:

Actar-D
Roca i Batlle 2
08023 Barcelona (España)
T +34 93 417 49 93
F +34 93 418 67 07
office@actar-d.com

Actar-D New York
158 Lafayette St. 5th floor
New York, NY 10013
T 212 966 2207
F 212 966 2214
officeusa@actar-d.com

Printed in the European Union
ISBN: 978-84-96954-37-3
D.L.: B-5927-2008